THE BIBLE IN 90 DAYS™
WHOLE-CHURCH CHALLENGE

PARTICIPANT'S GUIDE

THE BIBLE IN 90 DAYS™
WHOLE-CHURCH CHALLENGE

PARTICIPANT'S GUIDE

TED COOPER JR.

ZONDERVAN®

ZONDERVAN.com/
AUTHORTRACKER
follow your favorite authors

The Bible in 90 Days™: Whole Church Challenge Participant's Guide
Copyright © 2009 by Theodore W. Cooper Jr.

Requests for information should be addressed to:

Zondervan, *Grand Rapids, Michigan 49530*

ISBN 978-0-310-94184-2

Bible Background Sources:

Zondervan Handbook to the Bible, © 1999 Pat and David Alexander.

Zondervan NIV Study Bible, Copyright © 1985, 1995, 2002 by The Zondervan Corporation.

You Are Here in the Bible, Copyright © 2001, 2002, 2003 by Ted Cooper, Jr.

Interior design by Michelle Espinoza

Printed in the United States of America

09 10 11 12 13 14 • 23 22 21 20 19 18 17 16 15 14 13 12 11 10 9 8 7 6 5 4 3 2

CONTENTS

Welcome to The Bible in 90 Days™   7
Frequently Asked Questions   9
Discussion Group Rules of Engagement   11

Session 1   13
Session 2   20
Session 3   28
Session 4   37
Session 5   45
Session 6   53
Session 7   64
Session 8   72
Session 9   80
Session 10   90
Session 11   101
Session 12   111
Session 13   121
Session 14   130

The Bible in 90 Days™ *Listening Plan*   142

WELCOME TO
THE BIBLE IN 90 DAYS™

You are about to embark on a special journey.

The journey will start on the first page of the Bible and end on the last. You'll read 12 pages a day and finish in 90 days.

Others will be on this journey with you. You'll gather with them once a week to ask questions, share insights and hear a lesson drawn from your reading. You'll encourage them and they'll encourage you.

I took this journey for the first time six years ago. In the beginning, I was agnostic. Halfway through, I became a believer. Your experience will differ from mine, because you won't start this journey with the same background or needs. But whatever your background, be prepared for an extraordinary experience.

Reading every word of the Bible is not the norm, nor is doing so in such a short time frame. Something just happens when you do this. In your case, this "something" might be obvious, or maybe it won't become apparent for a while.

This curriculum and its accompanying resources will continue to evolve, so we invite your suggestions and comments. We've always believed that a critical ingredient in this curriculum's effectiveness is the godly guidance we receive from its participants and leaders ... people like you.

Please let us hear from you, either during or after your journey. We'll be praying for you.

Blessings,

Ted

Ted Cooper Jr.
Creator, *The Bible in 90 Days*™
(713)526–6800
www.biblein90days.org

FREQUENTLY ASKED QUESTIONS

Over time, a number of frequently asked questions have surfaced regarding this Bible reading program. Here are some of the more common queries and answers:

Q: Should I do anything before I start reading each day?

A: We recommend that you say a brief, silent prayer such as this: "Gracious Father, thank you for the gift I hold in my hands. May your Spirit fill me and interpret your precious words for me as I read. In your Son's name I pray. Amen."

Q: How much will I read each day?

A: Each day you'll read 12 pages in the *NIV Bible in 90 Days*. On Day 1 you start with page 1, on Day 2 you start with page 13. At the end of 90 days, you'll have read the Bible from cover to cover. We encourage you to do what you can to alleviate distractions so that you can reach your goal of reading each word attentively.

Q: When should I read?

A: That's completely up to you. Some will read first thing in the morning, before getting out of bed. Others will make it the last thing they do each night. Still others will read at various times during the day and/or night. Some will read their daily quota all in one sitting. Others will space their reading throughout the day, reading a page or two in several sittings. Try more than one approach; one of the benefits of doing this reading is becoming comfortable with reading your Bible at any time.

Q: What if I get behind?

A: Try your best not to get behind. But if you do, there is one *very important* rule about catching up: Do *not* skip any pages! There are two reasons for this rule: (1) If you skip anything, by definition you will not have read from *cover to cover*, which is an important part of this process. (2) If you skip anything, you are *unlikely* to go back and read what you skipped, so, again, you won't end up reading the entire Bible.

If you get behind, just read some extra pages each day until you've caught back up to the class.

Q: What if I get *way* behind?

A: If you happen to get more than a day or two behind, set aside a large block of time during one day—Sundays are particularly good for this—and just "plow through" the reading. This may seem more like a chore than a spiritual experience, but you will probably be surprised by the insights you glean from this. As importantly, after a day (or so) of reading this way, you'll be caught up! Remember, too, that God's work sometimes seems like, well, *work*. Reading the Bible from cover to cover *is* a challenge; however, when this challenge is met, you'll be glad that you persevered.

DISCUSSION GROUP RULES OF ENGAGEMENT

1. In each group, we've asked one or two people to serve as facilitators. These individuals will lead or guide the discussion, but will not *teach*.
2. Each small group member is *invited* to join into the discussion but is not *required* to do so. Even if a question is posed for everyone in the group to answer (for example, "Let's go around the table and find out what everyone thinks about ..."), each participant should feel free to remain silent on the subject. In such a case, someone abstaining might simply say, "Thank you, but I'd like to pass on answering that question."
3. Alternatively, please do not dominate the discussion. Discussion time is limited, so please be sure that everyone who wants to speak has the opportunity to do so.
4. Be sure to respect one another's beliefs, whether new to the Bible or a lifetime student. We are not here to correct or even guide anyone's interpretation of what is being read. Rather, we are here to encourage each person as he/she struggles with its meaning.
5. Begin and end your small group sessions — and return to the large group — promptly.

SESSION 1

A deeply religious man lived in a house by the river, but one day the banks burst and the house was flooded. As the water level rose alarmingly, the man climbed onto the roof of the house. A boat came by. "Climb aboard," called the captain.

"No, I shall stay here," said the man. "God will take care of me."

Twenty minutes later, with waters still rising, the man climbed onto the chimney. Another boat came past. "Jump aboard," said the captain.

"No, I shall stay here," said the man. "God will take care of me."

With the water up to the man's waist, a helicopter suddenly swooped down. "Quick!" shouted the pilot. "Climb aboard!"

"No, I shall stay here," said the man. "God will take care of me."

The water level continued to rise and soon the man was swept away from the chimney and drowned. Up in heaven, he sought out God. "I thought you said you would take care of me," he complained.

God said, "I sent you two boats and a helicopter. What more do you want?"

WHOLE GROUP DISCUSSION

1. Have you ever tried to read the entire Bible before? Why or why not?

2. If you have tried to read the Bible in its entirety, what challenges did you face in fulfilling your desire? Where did you start? How far did you get?

3. What have you found to be difficult and what have you found to be rewarding in your attempts to read the Bible regularly?

4. If you have successfully read the entire Bible before, what were the circumstances? What motivated you to keep at it? How satisfied were you with your accomplishment?

5. If you have started to read the Bible but have never completed your reading goal, what really kept you from finishing what you started?

6. What most excites you about the prospect of reading the entire Bible in 90 days?

7. Why do you believe it is important to read the entire Bible? What do you expect to discover in terms of practical living, spiritual growth, knowledge of history, or other areas?

VIDEO NOTES

VIDEO DISCUSSION NOTES

The creator of *The Bible in 90 Days* recommends a particular Bible because:

- ○ It's a translation (not a paraphrase) in _____ _____.

- ○ It's in _____ print so it's easier on your eyes.
- ○ It has few _____, so there are fewer distractions.
- ○ It's _____, so it looks less daunting to read, plus it's easy to carry.
- ○ In our discussions, we can refer to _____ rather than chapters and verses.

- • What should I do if I get behind in my reading? (Circle only one)

  a. Spend a little more time reading each day until I catch up and/ or set aside a special block of time to catch up
  b. Skip ahead
  c. Just quit

- • What if I am an atheist, an agnostic, or I don't believe this is the Word of God? Can I still join in?

_____

ON YOUR OWN BETWEEN SESSIONS

This Week's Reading Tips

- • You will be reading the Bible on your own. You can set your own schedule, but plan to read 12 pages a day (in the curriculum Bible, the *NIV Bible in 90 Days*) in order to keep up with the group. In 90 days, you will have accomplished your goal!
- • We'll meet together once a week for encouragement, fellowship, activities, accountability, group discussion and video lessons. But you'll read on your own, and the reading is the most important thing.
- • Try to read at different times to see what works best for you. Try reading in the morning and at night, or split your reading into different segments throughout the day and/or night. Try reading over a lunch hour, between meetings or while waiting in line.

- *Very important:* Understand what you can, but don't worry about the rest. You'll be getting more from your reading than you realize. This last point is so important that we'll repeat it several times in the next few weeks.

Before you start your reading, please indicate below how much of the Old Testament and New Testament you have read prior to taking this course.

	Old Testament	*New Testament*
None	○	○
A little	○	○
Less than half	○	○
Half	○	○
More than half	○	○
Almost all	○	○
All	○	○

BOOKS YOU'LL ENCOUNTER THIS WEEK
Genesis Overview

The adventure begins. God creates the universe and all things in it, providing an idyllic home for Adam and Eve. When the serpent tempts them to turn their back on God, the conflict for the rest of the Bible is set. God's intention for a relationship with humans is apparent throughout the Bible through the descriptions of his faithfulness and covenants with his chosen ones, even in the face of their unfaithfulness.

Exodus Overview

Four hundred years pass after the death of Joseph at the end of Genesis. The family of Abraham long ago lost the advantage of Joseph's significant political protection during their stay in Egypt. As a people, they are now slaves there. God proves he has not forgotten them by delivering them from slavery, building them up as his chosen ones in the eyes of the Egyptians and the world.

READ THIS WEEK

Pages 1–84 in the *NIV Bible in 90 Days* (Gen. 1:1—Ex. 40:38)

PERSONAL PROGRESS

If it is helpful to do so, use the following chart to record your reading progress this week. Establish a reading schedule that works well for you—then stick with it. Try to make it a habit to pray before you begin reading each day, asking God to use his Word to instruct and guide you.

✓	Day	Pages in the *NIV Bible in 90 Days*	Passage begins:
	1 (Today)	1–12	Genesis 1:1
	2	12–24	Genesis 17:1
	3	24–36	Genesis 28:20
	4	36–48	Genesis 40:12
	5	48–60	Exodus 1:1
	6	60–72	Exodus 15:19
	7	72–84	Exodus 29:1

PERSONAL READING NOTES

Take a moment to record the highlights — knowledge gained, puzzling questions, "aha! moments" — you experience during your reading this week.

SESSION 2

READING OUTLINE

Discuss Today:
> pages 1 – 84 in the *NIV Bible in 90 Days*
> (Gen. 1:1 — Ex. 40:38)

Reading for the Coming Week:
> pages 84 – 168 in the *NIV Bible in 90 Days*
> (Lev. 1:1 — Deut. 23:11)

Comedienne "Mrs. Hughes" tells of this exchange with her 15-year-old child after yet another argument.

Child: "Mom, why did you even have me, anyway?"

Mrs. Hughes: "Look, we decided to have a child. We had no idea that it would turn out to be *you*. Among other things, we were hoping for someone with a job!"

One difference between God and us is that he *does* know who his children will be. Yet he creates us and gives us a free will, despite that knowledge. A question we might ponder while reading the Bible from cover to cover is, "Knowing what he knows, why would God create each one of us? Why did God create me?"

SMALL GROUP DISCUSSION

[Group facilitator: Start your discussion group time by carefully reviewing the Discussion Group Rules of Engagement together, perhaps by selecting individuals to read each rule aloud. These are intended to help manage the discussions you'll be having in your group sessions.

If you have not already been introduced to each other, go around the group, stating your name and one thing everyone should know about you. Keep this brief, as you'll be particularly pressed for time this week, and you'll have time to get to know each other in the coming weeks.

Then, move through the following questions in the allotted time. Again, be aware that you'll have less time than normal for discussion this week, so do not get concerned if it seems a little rushed.]

1. What did you have to modify this week in order to do your Bible reading?

   ❏ TV watching
   ❏ Newspaper reading
   ❏ Work or school
   ❏ General time-wasting
   ❏ Exercise
   ❏ Sleep
   ❏ Other: _____

2. Check all that apply:

   ❏ I read mainly in the morning
   ❏ I read mainly in the afternoon
   ❏ I read mainly in the evening
   ❏ I prefer to tackle the entire daily reading in one sitting
   ❏ I prefer to break up my reading into smaller segments

3. Did you complete *all* of your reading for this week? If yes, was it easy to do? If no, what kept you from it?

4. Do you have a suggestion to help others who may be struggling with their reading?

5. Is the God you read about in Genesis and Exodus the God that you "know"? Did you ever get mad at him while you were reading? If so, when? Is that OK?

6. Let's face it: Adam and Eve blew it. The entire struggle of humankind derives from the fact that the first couple couldn't keep away from a piece of fruit. Have you ever blown it? What was the value of that experience?

7. As a group, try to recall the Ten Commandments by filling in the blanks below. Once the group is satisfied with the answers, go to Exodus 20:1 – 17 to check your work.

Concerning our relationship with God:

1. You shall have no other __God's__ before me.
2. You shall not make for yourself an __idol__.
3. You shall not __misuse__ the name of the Lord your God.
4. Remember the __Sabbath__ by keeping it __holy__.

Concerning our relationship with each other:

5. __Honor__ your __mother__ and __father__.
6. You shall not __murder__.
7. You shall not __commit adultry__.
8. You shall not __steal__.
9. You shall not give __false testimony__ against a neighbor.
10. You shall not __covet__ your neighbor's house, spouse or other possessions.

VIDEO NOTES

We are about to view a video lesson drawn from last week's reading. Please be aware that it is entirely possible that a video teacher will say something during this series with which you may *not* agree. If this occurs, simply set aside the issue in question and continue listening. The purpose of *The Bible in 90 Days* is *not* to promote a specific point of view, but rather to engage you in the reading.

VIDEO DISCUSSION NOTES

_____

_____

_____

_____

_____

_____

_____

_____

ON YOUR OWN BETWEEN SESSIONS

This Week's Reading Tips

- Remember what our mission is: "To read, attentively, every word of the Bible in 90 days."
- As you encounter repetition in the Bible, consider it an opportunity to more firmly plant important writings in your mind.
- Do *not* obsess with capturing everything that you're reading. Absorb what you can, and don't worry about the rest.
- If you have gotten behind in your reading, catch up by reading as long as necessary this Sunday.

The Scripture text in the Bible is accepted by many as the inspired Word of God. However, not everything in the Bible is Scripture text. Elements like chapter titles, book names, and chapter and verse numbers were added by scholars and printers in the sixteenth and seventeenth centuries to aid reading, studying and referencing.

Inspired	*Not Inspired*
Scripture text—every word	Book names
	Headlines
	Footnotes
	Chapters
	Sidebars
	Maps
	"Front" Matter
	"Back" Matter

BOOKS YOU'LL ENCOUNTER THIS WEEK
Leviticus Overview

This book of rules gives direction to the Levitical priests in the rituals necessary to maintain holiness for the children of Israel. While modern readers may marvel at the seeming harshness of some directives, it also includes God's earliest command to "love your neighbor as yourself."

Numbers Overview

At the beginning of this book, the Israelites number 603,550; at the end they number 601,730. What occurs in between is a lesson in the pitfalls of failing to submit to God and his plans.

Deuteronomy Overview

With the Israelites finally approaching entry into the promised land, many elements of the previous four books are revisited here, including the Ten Commandments. Moses gets to view the promised land from Mount Nebo but dies before his people enter it.

READ THIS WEEK

Pages 84–168 in the *NIV Bible in 90 Days* (Lev. 1:1 — Deut. 23:11)

PERSONAL PROGRESS

If it is helpful to do so, use the following chart to record your reading progress during the coming week. Establish a reading schedule that works well for you and stick with it. If you are behind in your reading, set aside extra time this week to catch up.

✓	Day	Pages in the *NIV Bible in 90 Days*	Passage begins:
	1 (Today) Thurs.	84–96	Leviticus 1:1
	2	96–108	Leviticus 14:33
	3	108–120	Leviticus 26:27
	4	120–132	Numbers 8:15
	5	132–144	Numbers 21:8
	6	144–156	Numbers 32:20
	7	157–168	Deuteronomy 8:1

PERSONAL READING NOTES

Take a moment to record the highlights—knowledge gained, puzzling questions, "aha! moments"—that you experience during your reading this week.

SESSION 3

READING OUTLINE

Discuss Today:
> pages 84–168 in the *NIV Bible in 90 Days*
> (Lev. 1:1—Deut. 23:11)

Reading for the Coming Week:
> pages 168–252 in the *NIV Bible in 90 Days*
> (Deut. 23:12—1 Sam. 28:19)

SMALL GROUP DISCUSSION

 **Warm-Up**

A young man asked God how long a million years was to him. God replied, "A million years to me is just like a single second in your time."

Then the young man asked God what a million dollars was to him. God replied, "A million dollars to me is just like a single penny to you."

Then the young man got his courage up and asked, "God, could I have one of your pennies?" God smiled and replied, "Certainly, just wait one second."

God perceives time differently than we do. Not only that, but God gives us time. So as some of us struggle to read 12 pages daily in our Bible, we may question whether we really have the time to read the Bible in 90 days. For most of us, I suspect God's answer to us would be, "Absolutely; I give you 24 hours each day." The question is not really whether or not we *have* the time, but how we choose to *use* it.

With this in mind, answer the following about your reading last week:

1. Are you reading the Bible instead of other things in your life or in addition to other things?

2. If you're struggling with your reading, are there activities that you can replace with Bible reading rather than reading in addition to your current activities? What activities can you eliminate?

3. What advice can others in the group give to those still trying to find their Bible reading rhythm?

 **Digging In**

4. Refer to Leviticus and fill in the five main sacrifices below:

Chapter	Sacrifice
Leviticus 1	
Leviticus 2	
Leviticus 3	
Leviticus 4	
Leviticus 5	

5. God lays out the elements and purposes of these offerings with some specificity. Is there too much detail here? What does this suggest about God's involvement in his people's lives?

6. What happens to Aaron's sons in Leviticus 10:1–2? What does this tell us about how God expects us to interact with him?

 **Applying It**

7. In Numbers we find God's people wandering in the wilderness for several decades—after failing to believe God would lead them to victory over the fearsome inhabitants of the promised land. Forty years and a whole generation waste away in the desert due to Israel's lack of belief. Have you ever experienced a similar delay or loss due to a similar lack of belief? Briefly describe. How can we apply this cautionary tale to our lives today?

8. We see in Deuteronomy that Moses dies after viewing the promised land, and that he never gets to enter it. After all the hardship he went through, does this seem a little unfair? From God's perspective, how might it be considered just?

9. Moses appears to accept this fate without argument. Which of the following, if any, would you be willing to labor in behalf of for most of your life without personally experiencing the payoff?

- ❏ God
- ❏ Spouse
- ❏ Children
- ❏ Career
- ❏ Ministry
- ❏ Volunteer organization
- ❏ Hobby
- ❏ Other: _____

10. For any of the above that you've checked, which are not currently a high priority in your daily life?

11. Is your daily reading of the Bible suggesting that you elevate anything noted in questions 9 and 10 to a higher priority? If so, what?

VIDEO NOTES

VIDEO DISCUSSION NOTES

_____

_____

_____

_____

_____

_____

_____

_____

ON YOUR OWN BETWEEN SESSIONS

This Week's Reading Tips

- Pay particular attention to the following people in your reading this week. How do these individuals interact with God? How faithful are they to God's will?
  - Joshua: Joshua, Rahab
  - Judges: Deborah, Gideon, Samson
  - Ruth: Ruth, Naomi, Boaz
  - 1 Samuel: Samuel, Saul, David

- Allocate some extra time this Sunday for reading. Use the extra time to catch up, if necessary. Or, see what it is like to get ahead.

✳ Good to Know ✳

- God and his holiness are the dominant themes of Leviticus. The word "holy" appears more times in Leviticus than in any other book of the Bible. And in just nine chapters of the book, God states "I am the LORD" 47 times (*NIV Study Bible*, study note for Lev. 18:2).
- The requirements for cleanliness and perfection found in the Old Testament laws are ultimately fulfilled in the person of Jesus Christ.
- The same Hebrew word used for an international treaty is also used for a covenant between God and his people (*Handbook*, 210). The Sinai covenant, the most important Old Testament covenant, was the key step in Israel becoming a nation. It followed the covenant God made with Noah (Gen. 9) and the two covenants God made with Abraham (Gen. 15; 17).

BOOKS YOU'LL ENCOUNTER THIS WEEK
Joshua Overview

Moses' former assistant becomes leader of the nation of Israel. The book celebrates the many victories that God brings to the Israelites under Joshua's leadership. At the same time, the failure of the people to follow completely God's plans plants the seeds for future failure.

Judges Overview

This book clearly delineates the impact of leaders who follow God from those who do not. Some of the favorite Biblical personalities from children's Sunday school are found here: Deborah, Gideon and Samson.

Ruth Overview

Ruth's story of faithfulness is remarkable in its own right, made more so considering she was from Moab, a nation considered an enemy of Israel. Ruth and Boaz are ancestors of Christ.

1 Samuel Overview

Samuel is not only a priest, prophet and judge, but a kingmaker. At God's behest, Samuel anoints Saul the first king of Israel after the people call for a king. God later directs Samuel to anoint Saul's successor, David, which sets up a series of conflicts between Saul and David.

READ THIS WEEK

Pages 168–252 in the *NIV Bible in 90 Days* (Deut. 23:12 — 1 Sam. 28:19)

PERSONAL PROGRESS

If it is helpful to do so, use the following chart to record your reading progress this week. Establish a reading schedule that works well for you — then stick with it.

✓	Day	Pages in the *NIV Bible in 90 Days*	Passage begins:
	1 (Today)	168–180	Deuteronomy 23:12
	2	180–192	Joshua 1:1
	3	192–204	Joshua 15:1
	4	205–216	Judges 3:28
	5	216–228	Judges 15:13
	6	228–240	1 Samuel 2:30
	7	240–252	1 Samuel 16:1

If you are behind in your reading, set aside extra time this week to catch up.

PERSONAL READING NOTES

Take a moment to record the highlights — knowledge gained, puzzling questions, "aha! moments" — you experience during your reading this week.

SESSION 4

READING OUTLINE

Discuss Today:
> pages 168–252 in the *NIV Bible in 90 Days*
> (Deut. 23:12—1 Sam. 28:19)

Reading for the Coming Week:
> pages 252–336 in the *NIV Bible in 90 Days*
> (1 Sam. 28:20—2 Kings 25:30)

SMALL GROUP DISCUSSION

 Warm-Up

In the early 1990s, H. Jackson Brown wrote *Life's Little Instruction Book*. The premise of the book was that his son was going off to college, and Dad couldn't go with him. Nevertheless, Dad wanted to share with his son some gems of wisdom that he had gleaned over the years. To be precise, Brown collected 511 gems of wisdom that were to guide his son's life. Here are some of the offerings:

- Learn to make great chili.
- Never buy a house without a fireplace.
- Overtip breakfast waitresses.
- Eat prunes.
- Be brave. Even if you're not, pretend to be. No one can tell the difference.
- Never go to bed with dirty dishes in the sink.

Evidently, unlike most college kids, his son responded enthusiastically to advice from his father—so enthusiastically, in fact, that the document made its way to a publisher and became a bestseller.

For all its commercial success, it's hard to know whether anyone was transformed by *Life's Little Instruction Book*. But the Bible is a different story. Billions of people have been changed by its message of hope and salvation. That said, here are some interesting statistics: In any given year, somewhere between 74 percent and 80 percent of American adults describe themselves as being Christian. Yet a study by Barna Research a few years ago showed that only 14 percent of American adults base their moral and ethical principles on the Bible.

1. Why do you think there is such a disconnect between modern Christians and the Bible?

2. How is your perception of the Bible changing as you are doing the daily readings?

3. What questions evolved from your reading this week?

 **Digging In**

4. Our reading shows us many instances when Israel only partially follows God's commands. What are some examples and what were the results?

5. Based on our reading to date, talk about what God tends to do when a society turns to him for help.

6. List the tragedies and unfortunate events that befall Naomi and Ruth in the book of Ruth. Does any good come from all of this?

Applying It

7. What are some contemporary examples of tragedy or hardship from which good has emerged?

8. As a group, take something from your reading this week and create a "life instruction." Be prepared to share it with the larger group.

VIDEO NOTES

VIDEO DISCUSSION NOTES

_____

_____

_____

_____

_____

_____

_____

_____

_____

_____

ON YOUR OWN BETWEEN SESSIONS

This Week's Reading Tips

- If you are unfamiliar with the books in this week's reading, you may become very confused. There are several reasons for this, including:
  - Many new people and names are introduced that can be hard to distinguish from one another.
  - Some events are described more than once.
  - The kings of Israel and Judah are handled in rapid-fire succession.

- To minimize confusion:
  - While continuing to read attentively every word, focus your attention in a manner that allows you to notice patterns of behavior by the various kings. For most of the kings, their *pattern* of behavior

rather than the *specifics* of their behavior are key. The kings who distinguish themselves will be pretty clear to you.

○ As you read 1 Kings and 2 Kings, fill in the diagram below.

Patterns in 1 and 2 Kings

Instructions: As you read 1 Kings and 2 Kings, mark the diagram below with a check next to the names of the kings who do "right in the eyes of the LORD" and an X next to the names of the kings who don't.

Northern king (Israel)	Does or does not do right in the eyes of the Lord	Southern king (Judah)	Does or does not do right in the eyes of the Lord
Jeroboam I		Rehoboam	
Nadab		Abijah	
Baasha		Asa	
Elah		Jehoshaphat	
Zimri		Jehoram	
Tibni		Ahaziah	
Omri		Athaliah (Queen)	
Ahab		Joash	
Ahaziah		Amaziah	
Joram		Azariah (Uzziah)	
Jehu		Jotham	
Jehoahaz		Ahaz	
Joash/Jehoash		Hezekiah	
Jeroboam II		Manasseh	
Zechariah		Amon	
Shallum		Josiah	
Menahem		Jehoahaz	
Pekahiah		Jehoiakim	
Pekah		Jehoiachin	
Hoshea		Zedekiah	

BOOKS YOU'LL ENCOUNTER THIS WEEK

2 Samuel Overview

David becomes king over Israel and Judah. As much as David is "God's man," even he falls short of perfection. Nevertheless, while David does suffer consequences for his failings, his faith in God remains constant.

1 Kings Overview

The book opens with the reign of Solomon, a time when Israel enjoys a great deal of influence, wealth and worldwide recognition. Yet, even as the world's wisest man, Solomon is corrupted by worldly matters and the faiths of his wives and concubines. At his death the kingdom becomes divided.

2 Kings Overview

Continues the account of the kings of the divided kingdom through the fall of Jerusalem.

READ THIS WEEK

Pages 252–336 in the *NIV Bible in 90 Days* (1 Sam. 28:20—2 Kings 25:30)

PERSONAL PROGRESS

If it is helpful to do so, use the following chart to record your reading progress this week. Establish a reading schedule that works well for you—then stick with it.

✓	Day	Pages in the *NIV Bible in 90 Days*	Passage begins:
	1 (Today)	252–264	1 Samuel 28:20
	2	264–276	2 Samuel 12:11
	3	277–288	2 Samuel 22:19
	4	288–300	1 Kings 7:38
	5	300–312	1 Kings 16:21
	6	312–324	2 Kings 4:38
	7	324–336	2 Kings 15:27

If you are behind in your reading, set aside extra time this week to catch up.

PERSONAL READING NOTES

Take a moment to record the highlights — knowledge gained, puzzling questions, "aha! moments" — you experience during your reading this week.

SESSION 5

READING OUTLINE

Discuss Today:
pages 252–336 in the *NIV Bible in 90 Days*
(1 Sam. 28:20 — 2 Kings 25:30)
Reading for the Coming Week:
pages 336–420 in the *NIV Bible in 90 Days*
(1 Chron. 1:1 — Neh. 13:14)

SMALL GROUP DISCUSSION

 **Warm-Up**

Two men dressed in pilot's uniforms walk up the aisle of the plane. Both are wearing dark glasses, one is using a guide dog and the other is tapping his way along the aisle with a cane. At the cockpit, the door closes and the engines start up. The passengers begin glancing nervously around, searching for some sign that this is just a practical joke.

The plane moves faster and faster down the runway and the people sitting in the window seats realize they are heading straight for the water at the edge of the airport. As it begins to look as though the plane will crash into the water, panicked screams fill the cabin.

Just at that moment, the plane lifts smoothly into the air. The passengers relax and laugh sheepishly, and soon all retreat into their magazines, secure in the knowledge that the plane is in good hands.

In the cockpit, one of the pilots turns to the other and says, "You know, Bob, one of these days, they're gonna scream too late and we're all gonna die."

1. We'll get to the specifics below, but, as you experienced 2 Samuel and 1 and 2 Kings, did you get the feeling that many of the "pilots" of the northern and southern kingdoms were blind? Why do you think God allowed them to be the pilots?

2. We've all seen the bumper sticker that says, "If God is your copilot, switch seats." Without discussing specific candidates or political parties, what might happen if our political leaders took this advice?

 **Digging In**

3. How does the Lord use the prophet Nathan in 2 Samuel 12?

4. Does David immediately realize the significance of Nathan's story about the rich man?

5. What does David's response in 2 Samuel 12:13 say about his relationship with God?

6. What were the consequences of David's sins?

7. Last week we encouraged you to do a quick assessment of the northern and southern kings as you read 1 and 2 Kings. Referring back to page 42 in this participant's guide, what patterns emerge?

Applying It

8. We are all sinners. We all fall short. So it is reassuring to see the grace that God demonstrates toward humanity when we fail. It is also sobering to realize that there often are consequences, even in the midst of grace. At this point in your reading, are you focused more on God being a God of grace or a God of consequences? How might you use this focus to guide a decision you need to make in the near future? Either share with the group or reflect on this privately.

9. Is there an "aha" triggered by your reading this week that you can immediately apply to your life?

VIDEO NOTES

VIDEO DISCUSSION NOTES

_____

_____

_____

_____

_____

_____

_____

_____

_____

_____

_____

ON YOUR OWN BETWEEN SESSIONS

This Week's Reading Tips

- This week we blaze past the halfway point in the Old Testament. Enjoy this accomplishment!
- Remember that while 1 and 2 Chronicles repeat previously reported events, the editorial comment is somewhat different. Focus on the difference in emphasis.

Looking Forward to Jesus

Solomon appears in many ways as a Christlike figure. He is portrayed as the wisest man in the world, one who had access to vast resources. In a later age, he would have been referred to as a Renaissance man: among other things, he is also a builder and poet. But like his father, David, Solomon falls woefully short of Christ in his humanness. Nevertheless, Solomon gives us an imperfect peek at the One to come.

Ezra plays a critical role in the worthy effort to get postexilic Hebrews to be true to God's law. Unfortunately, some followers carry the teachings too far. By Christ's time, these types of followers are known as the Pharisees.

BOOKS YOU'LL ENCOUNTER THIS WEEK

1 Chronicles Overview

Covers much of the same ground as 2 Samuel. This book was written *after* Judah returns from exile and is intended as an encouragement to the returnees. As such, its emphasis is on the more positive events/aspects of the reigns covered.

2 Chronicles Overview

Covers much of the same ground as 1 and 2 Kings. Like 1 Chronicles, it was written *after* Judah returns from exile and is intended as an encouragement to the returnees.

Ezra Overview

When Cyrus became king of Persia, the Lord led him to free the exiles to return to Jerusalem. Ezra, a teacher "well versed in the Law of Moses," arrives several decades later to discover that many from Judah have been intermarrying with the neighboring peoples.

Nehemiah Overview

Whereas Ezra is a teacher and scribe, Nehemiah is a leader. The book of Nehemiah celebrates the rebuilding of Jerusalem's walls against significant odds. The behavior of the residents when Nehemiah is in residence and when he is not harkens back to the era of the Judges.

READ THIS WEEK

Pages 336–420 in the *NIV Bible in 90 Days* (1 Chron. 1:1—Neh. 13:14)

PERSONAL PROGRESS

If it is helpful to do so, use the following chart to record your reading progress this week. Establish a reading schedule that works well for you—then stick with it.

✓	Day	Pages in the *NIV Bible in 90 Days*	Passage begins:
	1 (Today)	336–348	1 Chronicles 1:1
	2	349–360	1 Chronicles 10:1
	3	360–372	1 Chronicles 24:1
	4	372–384	2 Chronicles 7:11
	5	384–396	2 Chronicles 23:16
	6	396–408	2 Chronicles 35:16
	7	408–420	Nehemiah 1:1

If you are behind in your reading, set aside extra time this week to catch up.

PERSONAL READING NOTES

Take a moment to record the highlights — knowledge gained, puzzling questions, "aha! moments" — you experience during your reading this week.

SESSION 6

READING OUTLINE

Discuss Today:
    pages 336–420 in the *NIV Bible in 90 Days*
    (1 Chron. 1:1 — Neh. 13:14)
Reading for the Coming Week:
    pages 420–504 in the *NIV Bible in 90 Days*
    (Neh. 13:15 – Ps. 89:13)

SMALL GROUP DISCUSSION

 **Warm-Up**

There is an old story about three sons who left home, went out on their own, and prospered. Getting back together, they bragged to each other about the gifts they were able to give their elderly mother.

The first said, "I built a big house for our mother." The second said, "I sent her a Mercedes with a driver." The third said, "I've got you both beat. You remember how Mom enjoys reading the Bible? And you remember that she doesn't see very well anymore? I sent her a remarkable parrot that recites the entire Bible. It took elders in my church 12 years to teach him. He's one of a kind. Mom just has to name chapter and verse, and the parrot recites it."

Soon after, Mom sent letters of thanks to her sons: "Milton," she wrote to one son, "the house you built is too big. I live in only one room, but I have to clean the whole house." "Gerald," she wrote to the second, "I am too old to travel. I stay most of the time at home, so I rarely use the Mercedes. And the driver is so rude!" "Dearest Donald," she wrote to her third son, "you have the good sense to know what your mother likes. The chicken was delicious."

Clearly, the mother enjoyed the present from her third son, though presumably not in the manner he intended!

1. Based on your reading so far, what are three or four ways in which you think God intends for us to benefit from the Scriptures?

Benefits of Scripture Reading	Are you currently taking advantage of this intended benefit?
God reveals himself to us.	
God instructs us regarding how to live.	
God demonstrates his love for us.	
God gave the Bible to us so that we could have a ready reference to answer many of our questions about Christian living.	

- Did you enjoy the Bible in these ways before your current reading?
- Have you enjoyed the Bible in these ways while completing this current reading?
- Do you expect to enjoy the Bible in these ways after you have completed this goal?

2. What questions evolved from your reading this week?

3. Imagine what the temple might have looked like. What would have been most striking to you? What does Scripture suggest about Solomon's care in building the Lord's temple?

4. God responds to the temple and Solomon's dedication by saying three things. Paraphrase each of his statements in a sentence or two:

Scripture	Your paraphrase
2 Chron. 7:11 – 16	
2 Chron. 7:17 – 18	
2 Chron. 7:19 – 22	

 **Applying It**

5. In his life and writings, Ezra adamantly encouraged people to follow the Law. Think of someone you can encourage this week to read or study the Bible. Who is it? How can you encourage this person? How would this person benefit from the experience? How can you break through any barriers that may be standing in the way of talking to this person?

6. List and describe some of Nehemiah's leadership qualities. Would they be relevant for today's leaders? Did you learn anything from Nehemiah that you could add to your own leadership toolbox? If so, what?

LARGE GROUP ACTIVITY
Recapping the Events of the Old Testament

- God creates everything, including humans, to live in perfect relationship with him.
- God places Adam and Eve in the Garden of Eden, makes them responsible for overseeing the animals and working the land, and gives them unfettered access to the entire Garden of Eden except for one tree: the tree of the knowledge of good and evil.
- Adam and Eve are enticed, tempted by the serpent, and then fall to temptation by eating from the tree that God had told them to leave alone.
- God responds by punishing them. He makes them mortal (which they weren't before), and he banishes them from the Garden of Eden.
- But things don't go very well outside the Garden. A lot of begetting goes on, but people soon forget about God. So God chooses a righteous man, has him build an ark and load his family, his in-laws and a sampling of animals into the ark. Then God floods the world, killing all other living beings.
- Noah's family exits the ark, begets some more, and soon a group of people decides to build a tower toward the sky in yet another attempt to become like God. God confuses their language, and they then scatter all over the earth.
- It is at this point that we start to get the idea that there might be a plan for rescuing at least some humans from the mess that was started in the Garden of Eden.
- God chooses Abraham as the leader of a chosen people, makes certain promises to them, and keeps those promises. Then God starts

doing some things to show his power and to give the people some confidence in his ability to do things.

- For instance, he leads them out of slavery in Egypt. He gives them 10 laws to live by. He promises that they will soon live together in a fertile land as his people, and he promises that he will overthrow the big, hulking inhabitants of that land.
- But the people don't have enough faith. They may want to believe, but a negative report from a group of spies leaves them fearful and doubtful.
- So God punishes them; he has them wander in the wilderness for 38 years, until all but two of the original group that he had rescued from Egypt are dead.
- After this time, God prepares them to enter the promised land. Through Moses, he delivers explicit instructions on what they are to do and how they are to do it. He also warns them what will happen if they don't follow through.
- As we know, the people do enter the promised land, led by Joshua, and God helps them defeat the inhabitants of that land. However, contrary to God's direct orders, they fail to completely wipe out their enemies.
- This last reality leads to trouble, as God's people intermarry with the pagan peoples of the new land. This leads the people away from God and toward pagan gods. Their pure belief becomes corrupt as other gods figure into their theology and practice. This is indirect conflict with the very first commandment: "You shall have no other gods before me."
- At this point we're arriving at the age of the judges. The further the people turn from God, the worse their circumstances become. And so begins a negative cycle of events: First, God lets Israel's enemies overrun them. Then they plead with God, and he raises up a strong, God-fearing leader, empowering that individual to carry out his deliverance. After that, Israel is at peace for 40 to 80 years. But the people turn away when they don't have that strong, God-fearing leader. Their circumstances deteriorate again, and the cycle continues.
- Finally the people plead for a king so they can be like all the other nations. God has already warned them—way back in Deuteronomy—

that a human king is not a good idea. But he finally relents and tells Samuel to search for the man he has selected as their king.

- King Saul starts well but ends poorly, and the glory years of Israel then ensue through the reigns of David and Solomon. But in their humanness, they demonstrate some real faults. In the end, they lay the groundwork for a political kingdom that is tragically short-lived. The kingdom splits into Israel and Judah.

- None of the 20 kings of Israel does what is right in the eyes of God. And God responds by letting Assyria defeat Israel in 722 B.C. The scattered survivors disappear from recorded history.

- Of the 19 kings and 1 queen of Judah, only a handful do what is right in the eyes of God. The kings who forget God lead the people astray, and God allows the Babylonians to destroy Judah and exile its people to Babylon.

VIDEO NOTES

VIDEO DISCUSSION NOTES

_____

_____

_____

_____

_____

_____

_____

_____

_____

ON YOUR OWN BETWEEN SESSIONS

This Week's Reading Tips

The messages from Psalms are timeless, making it one of the best-loved, most-read books of the Bible. As you read through the psalms at our rapid pace, mark the ones that seem particularly relevant to you, so that you can return to them for further perusal at a later date.

Looking Forward to Jesus

Written as many as 1000 years before Jesus' birth, several of the psalms appear to point to the coming Messiah. These include psalms 2, 8, 16, 22, 45, 69, 72, 89, 100, 118 and 132.

The New Testament validates the prophetic nature of many of the psalms. As the Gospel of John indicates, Psalm 22 depicts the crucifixion of Christ in detail, hundreds of years before the event.

✳ Good to Know ✳

Seventy-three psalms are said to be "of David."

C. S. Lewis said: "The psalms are poems, and poems intended to be sung: not doctrinal treatises, not even sermons ... They must be read as poems if they are to be understood ... Otherwise we will miss what is in them and think we see what is not."

BOOKS YOU'LL ENCOUNTER THIS WEEK

Esther Overview

Describing events several decades prior to those described in Nehemiah, the events in Esther may have enabled those in Nehemiah.

Job Overview

Scholars believe that Job was a contemporary of the patriarchs. In this philosophical discourse, God allows Satan to test Job, then clears up some misconceptions of Job and his friends.

Psalms Overview

One of the best-loved books of the Bible, Psalms is a collection of 150 hymns and poems, authored over a period of hundreds of years. As you move through the Psalms at your normal *The Bible in 90 Days* reading pace, mark the ones you want revisit at a later date in order to appreciate them more fully.

READ THIS WEEK

Pages 420–504 in the *NIV Bible in 90 Days* (Neh. 13:15 — Ps. 89:13)

PERSONAL PROGRESS

If it is helpful to do so, use the following chart to record your reading progress this week. Establish a reading schedule that works well for you — then stick with it.

✓	Day	Pages in the *NIV Bible in 90 Days*	Passage begins:
	1 (Today)	420 – 433	Nehemiah 13:15
	2	433 – 444	Job 8:1
	3	444 – 456	Job 25:1
	4	456 – 468	Job 42:1
	5	468 – 480	Psalm 25:1
	6	480 – 492	Psalm 45:15
	7	492 – 504	Psalm 69:22

If you are behind in your reading, set aside extra time this week to catch up.

PERSONAL READING NOTES

Take a moment to record highlights—knowledge gained, puzzling questions, "aha! moments"—you experience during your reading this week.

SESSION 7

READING OUTLINE

Discuss Today:
> pages 420–504 in the *NIV Bible in 90 Days*
> (Neh. 13:15 — Ps. 89:13)

Reading for the Coming Week:
> pages 504–588 in the *NIV Bible in 90 Days*
> (Ps. 89:14–Isa. 13:22)

SMALL GROUP DISCUSSION

 **Warm-Up**

Seen on a bumper sticker: *"Most people want to serve God, but only in an advisory capacity."*

1. This week you read Job, a book in which a collection of Job's friends comfort him by advising him on the reasons for his distress. Did you agree with any of the arguments made by Job's friends? If so, which ones?

2. Have you ever felt a bit like Job? When you are distressed, where have you historically gone for solutions? Check all that apply. Circle the one you go to most often.

   ❏ Friends
   ❏ Family members
   ❏ A bar
   ❏ Prayer

❏ Self-help book
❏ The gym
❏ The Bible
❏ Other: _____

3. After reading the Bible for several weeks, do you think your search for solutions will change? Why or why not?

Digging In

4. Did you notice that God is never mentioned in the book of Esther? Nevertheless, there are examples that his hand is at work throughout. What are some examples?

5. Job is often associated with the terms "suffering" or "patience." Build a case supporting the contention that this book is really about "faith."

6. Let one or two people in the group share their favorite psalm. What is particularly striking or significant about your psalm?

 **Applying It**

7. How does God answer Job's questions? Does he answer the way you want him to answer? Does his response impact the way you will make decisions in the future?

8. In last week's Reading Tips, we recommended that you mark the psalms that you want to go back to, the ones you want to spend more time reading and studying. Which of those psalms, or the ones just mentioned by your fellow small group members, has changed the way you will communicate with God in the future?

9. How did this week's reading impact your thoughts on a current event or personal experience?

VIDEO NOTES

VIDEO DISCUSSION NOTES

_____

_____

_____

_____

_____

_____

_____

_____

_____

ON YOUR OWN BETWEEN SESSIONS

This Week's Reading Tips

You will read four very different kinds of books this week. Some of these books lend themselves more readily to this kind of reading than others. Find a rhythm that works for each book, and stick with the reading. Absorb what you can, and don't worry about the rest.

Looking Forward to Jesus

Foretelling Christ's birth:

Therefore the Lord himself will give you a sign: The virgin will be with child and will give birth to a son, and will call him Immanuel. Isaiah 7:14

Foretelling Christ as Savior

Do not be afraid; you will not suffer shame. Do not fear disgrace; you will not be humiliated. You will forget the shame of your youth and remember no more the reproach of your widowhood. For your Maker is your husband—the LORD Almighty is his name—the Holy One of Israel is your Redeemer; he is called the God of all the earth. Isaiah 54:4–6

BOOKS YOU'LL ENCOUNTER THIS WEEK

Proverbs Overiew

This is a book of pithy sayings that highlight *general principles* about how to live wisely.

Ecclesiastes Overview

This book, written by a wise "teacher," contains a discourse on the meaninglessness of life, even for those who live lives of privilege. With this bleak stage set, the Teacher concludes the book by pointing to the only true source of meaning and hope.

Song of Songs Overview

Where Ecclesiastes contains some depressing thoughts, Song of Songs is an optimistic celebration of love. Various interpretations see it as a love poem between lovers, a representation of Christ's love for the Church, or an illustration of God's love for his people. The imagery is some of the most sexually graphic found in the Scriptures.

Isaiah Overview

Prophesying during the reigns of the later kings of Judah, Isaiah warns friends and foes alike. He foretells the coming of Christ, praises the Lord's faithfulness and offers comfort for God's people.

READ THIS WEEK

Pages 504–588 in the *NIV Bible in 90 Days* (Ps. 89:14 — Isa. 13:22)

PERSONAL PROGRESS

If it is helpful to do so, use the following chart to record your reading progress this week. Establish a reading schedule that works well for you — then stick with it.

✓	Day	Pages in the *NIV Bible in 90 Days*	Passage begins:
	1 (Today)	504–517	Psalm 89:14
	2	517–528	Psalm 109:1
	3	528–540	Psalm 135:1
	4	540–552	Proverbs 7:1
	5	552–564	Proverbs 20:22
	6	564–576	Ecclesiastes 3:1
	7	577–588	Isaiah 1:1

If you are behind in your reading, set aside extra time this week to catch up.

PERSONAL READING NOTES

Take a moment to record the highlights—knowledge gained, puzzling questions, "aha! moments"—you experience during your reading this week.

SESSION 8

READING OUTLINE

Discuss Today:
pages 504–588 in the *NIV Bible in 90 Days*
(Ps. 89:14—Isa. 13:22)

Reading for the Coming Week:
pages 588–672 in the *NIV Bible in 90 Days*
(Isa. 14:1—Jer. 33:22)

SMALL GROUP DISCUSSION

 **Warm-Up**

Here are two passages that probably few of us ever expected to read in the Bible:

Better to live in a desert
than with a quarrelsome and ill-tempered wife.
Proverbs 21:19

As a dog returns to its vomit,
so a fool repeats his folly.
Proverbs 26:11

1. How do you respond to the proverbs above?

2. Why do you think they are included in the Scriptures?

3. Individually—or as a group—write in the space below a two-line proverb expressing a woman's version of the first proverb above.

 **Digging In**

4. (Optional) There are four types of proverbs:
    a. Synonymous—the second line repeats the first line in a little different way
    b. Antithetical—the second line is contrary to the first line
    c. Synthetic—the second line adds to the idea of the first line
    d. Comparative—a truth is explained relative to some experience or something in nature

    Identify the following proverbs as one of the types from above:

    _____ *The truly righteous man attains life,*
    but he who pursues evil goes to his death.
        Proverbs 11:19

    _____ *As a door turns on its hinges,*
    so a sluggard turns on his bed.
        Proverbs 26:14.

    _____ *Whoever flatters his neighbor*
    is spreading a net for his feet.
        Proverbs 29:5

    _____ *He who heeds discipline shows the way to life,*
    but whoever ignores correction leads others astray.
        Proverbs 10:17

_____ *He who brings trouble on his family will inherit only wind,*
and the fool will be servant to the wise.
  Proverbs 11:29

_____ *The Righteous One takes note of the house of the wicked*
and brings the wicked to ruin.
  Proverbs 21:12

_____ *Better to live in the desert*
than with a quarrelsome and ill-tempered wife.
  Proverbs 21:19

5. If your small group is part of a larger group that meets together, you will have the opportunity to share with the larger group either the proverb you wrote in (3) above or your favorite proverb. Indicate your choice below:

 **Applying It**

6. Ecclesiastes disputes any notion that life has any meaning apart from God. Can you really accept this on an intellectual level? On an emotional one? Name something you will change about your life as a result of this new, or newly reiterated, point of view.

7. Throughout his life, the prophet Isaiah is God's advocate before the kings of Judah. Would you be willing to be God's advocate before a president of the United States? Who would you preach to, if led by God to do so? How might you override any personal barriers that might make this a challenge for you?

8. Pick a short psalm that you like and vow to commit it to memory this week. Write the psalm on a separate piece of paper, and take it with you throughout the week, rereading it as many times as you can.

   If you've never memorized Scripture before, this will give you a taste. Once you finish reading through the entire Bible, you might want to start setting aside some time each week to memorize selected verses.

VIDEO NOTES

VIDEO DISCUSSION NOTES

_____

_____

_____

_____

_____

_____

_____

_____

_____

ON YOUR OWN BETWEEN SESSIONS

This Week's Reading Tips

The books of the prophets are challenging even to Biblical scholars, so be prepared to "press on" after reading passages that you don't quite fully understand.

The book of Isaiah can be particularly challenging, because:

1. It contains a collection of visions and prophecies relating to various times.

2. It is not always easy to follow — partly because we are unfamiliar with the language and ways of the prophets and visionaries, and partly because we do not know on what basis (chronological order, topical order, etc.) the material was assembled.

BOOKS YOU'LL ENCOUNTER THIS WEEK
Jeremiah Overview

Jeremiah is a reluctant prophet. So much so that he is commonly referred to as the weeping prophet. Among other challenges, God calls on him to tell the people of Judah that God will allow their capture by Nebuchadnezzar and their subsequent exile in Babylon. But, in the midst of such woe, Jeremiah's book also points to the coming Christ.

READ THIS WEEK

Pages 588–672 in the *NIV Bible in 90 Days* (Isa. 14:1 — Jer. 33:22)

PERSONAL PROGRESS

If it is helpful to do so, use the following chart to record your reading progress this week. Establish a reading schedule that works well for you — then stick with it.

✓	Day	Pages in the *NIV Bible in 90 Days*	Passage begins:
	1 (Today)	588–600	Isaiah 14:1
	2	600–612	Isaiah 29:1
	3	612–624	Isaiah 41:19
	4	624–636	Isaiah 52:13
	5	636–648	Isaiah 66:19
	6	648–660	Jeremiah 10:14
	7	660–672	Jeremiah 23:9

If you are behind in your reading, set aside extra time this week to catch up.

PERSONAL READING NOTES

Take a moment to record the highlights—knowledge gained, puzzling questions, "aha! moments"—you experience during your reading this week.

SESSION 9

READING OUTLINE

Discuss Today:
>pages 588–672 in the *NIV Bible in 90 Days*
>(Isa. 14:1—Jer. 33:22)

Reading for the Coming Week:
>pages 672–756 in the *NIV Bible in 90 Days*
>(Jer. 33:23—Dan. 8:27)

SMALL GROUP DISCUSSION

 **Warm-Up**

Part of what happens to us as we experience the Bible as we have in the past eight weeks is that we become transformed in the process — transformed from our *before* person to our *after* person. For some of us the transformation will be radical; for others, very gradual; for still others, somewhere in between. So let's take a few minutes to assess ourselves.

1. How have you changed in the last eight weeks? Is it simply a matter of modifying your routine a bit, or do you sense something deeper and more significant going on? What might that be?

2. If you don't sense a change in yourself, does someone in your family or your group sense anything different about you? Or, is it possible that you are resisting changes that God is inviting you to make? If so, can you or someone in your group think of how you might overcome this resistance?

 **Digging In**

Biblical prophecy is not just about predicting future events. In fact, much of it serves a distinctly different purpose: It provides an inspired perspective on current events. Keep this in mind as you discuss questions 3 and 4.

3. Use a word or brief phrase to capture Jeremiah's description of godly people in the following verses:

   7:23
   9:24
   22:16
   24:7
   29:11

   Do you agree with this list? What would you add to or subtract from it?

4. What attributes of God are found in the following passages from Jeremiah?

   27:4–6
   31:1–4
   31:34b
   32:40

Name at least two attributes of God not described in the passages above. Do you now have a comprehensive picture of God? Why or why not?

 **Applying It**

5. Isaiah 58 describes "true fasting." Many Christians today have *never* fasted, much less fasted in a way intended to please God. Have you ever fasted? If so, what was it like? If not, would you consider doing so? (You can take your first step toward fasting now by writing "Fast" on your "What Might Be Next for Me" list on page 134 of this participant's guide.)

VIDEO NOTES

VIDEO DISCUSSION NOTES

_____

_____

_____

_____

_____

_____

_____

_____

_____

ON YOUR OWN BETWEEN SESSIONS

This Week's Reading Tips

Here are some of the major hurdles we encounter when reading the books of the prophets:

1. Knowing when the prophet is writing
2. Knowing to whom the prophet is writing
3. Knowing the circumstances of the prophet's audience
4. Knowing whether the prophet is describing a current event/situation or one that the prophet is foretelling

The chart "Putting the Prophets in Their Place" (pages 85–87) should help you with the first three hurdles described above. Keep it nearby while reading during the next few weeks.

As for the last hurdle, sometimes it is easy to tell, but many times it isn't. Welcome to the books of the prophets! Just remember, absorb what you can, and don't worry about the rest.

Good news: The next stop after the books of the prophets is the New Testament. At that point, you'll be in the home stretch. Keep reading!

Putting the Prophets in Their Place			
Book	**Era**	**Audience**	**Theme(s)**
Isaiah (chs. 1–39)	Pre-exile c. 700 B.C.?	Judah	Judgment against Judah and Israel; prophecies of promise and blessing; judgments against nations
Isaiah (chs. 40–55)	Exile c. 680 B.C.?	Judah	Deliverance and restoration of Israel; the servant's ministry; God's call to salvation
Isaiah (chs. 56–66)	Uncertain	Judah	Condemnation of wicked; worship; restoration; everlasting deliverance, everlasting judgment
Jeremiah	Pre-exile 7th/6th century B.C.	Judah	Warnings and exhortations; his suffering; fall of Jerusalem; judgment against nations
Lamentations (Jeremiah)	Pre-exile/exile c. 580 B.C.	Judah	Laments over destruction of Jerusalem

Book	Era	Audience	Theme(s)
Ezekiel	Exile 6th century B.C.	Jews in Babylon	God's sovereignty over creation, people, nations and history; God's holiness; judgment against Judah and pagan nations; God's future work in history
Daniel	Exile c. 530 B.C.	Jews in Babylon	Prayer; spiritual warfare; living by God's standards in a hostile environment; God's sovereignty
Hosea	Pre-exile 8th century B.C.	Israel	Just as Hosea is betrayed by his beloved, God is betrayed by his beloved Israel; loving commitment can overcome betrayal
Joel	Pre-exile Uncertain	Judah	God's people have a choice: keep doing wrong and be judged, or repent and receive God's forgiveness and salvation
Amos	Pre-exile 8th century B.C.	Israel	Israel ignores what matters to God—justice, compassion and worship from the heart—and God's impending judgment
Obadiah	Pre-exile c. 587 B.C.	Edom	Edomites, who treated Israel unjustly, now face God's anger

Book	Era	Audience	Theme(s)
Jonah	Pre-exile 8th century B.C.	Assyria	God's forgiveness of us; our need to forgive others
Micah	Pre-exile 8th century B.C.	Judah	God's judgment for idolatry and oppression; his mercy for the obedient; our need to show mercy; the coming Messiah
Nahum	Pre-exile 7th century B.C.	Assyria	The judgment of Assyria and its capital, Nineveh
Habakkuk	Pre-exile 7th century B.C.	Judah	Is God ignoring evil, or will he settle the score?
Zephaniah	Pre-exile 7th century B.C.	Judah	Judgment day is coming; closing promise
Haggai	Post-exile 6th century B.C.	Jews in Jerusalem	God's blessings, and what the Jews did to hinder them; Jews rebuild the temple
Zechariah	Post-exile 6th/5th (?) century B.C.	Jews in Jerusalem	God's encouragement to exiles who return from Babylon; prophecies about the coming Messiah; salvation
Malachi	Post-exile 5th/4th (?) century B.C.	Jews in Jerusalem	God's readiness to replace the old covenant with the new; prophecies about the Messiah, who will usher in the new covenant

[Source: Zondervan Handbook of the Bible, 411, and the author.]

BOOKS YOU'LL ENCOUNTER THIS WEEK
Lamentations Overview

Poetic laments concerning the destruction of Jerusalem.

Ezekiel Overview

Ezekiel's initial prophecies warn of the fall of Jerusalem. After the fall, he offers oracles of hope.

Daniel Overview

Daniel and his three friends are exemplary representatives of God while in exile in Babylon. While there, Daniel pens a number of long-range prophecies.

READ THIS WEEK

Pages 672–756 in the *NIV Bible in 90 Days* (Jer. 33:23—Dan. 8:27)

PERSONAL PROGRESS

If it is helpful to do so, use the following chart to record your reading progress this week. Establish a reading schedule that works well for you—then stick with it.

✓	Day	Pages in the *NIV Bible in 90 Days*	Passage begins:
	1 (Today)	672–684	Jeremiah 33:23
	2	684–696	Jeremiah 48:1
	3	696–708	Lamentations 2:1
	4	708–720	Ezekiel 12:21
	5	720–732	Ezekiel 23:40
	6	733–744	Ezekiel 36:1
	7	745–756	Ezekiel 47:13

If you are behind in your reading, set aside extra time this week to catch up.

PERSONAL READING NOTES

Take a moment to record the highlights—knowledge gained, puzzling questions, "aha! moments"—you experience during your reading this week.

SESSION 10

READING OUTLINE

Discuss Today:
pages 672–756 in the *NIV Bible in 90 Days*
(Jer. 33:23 — Dan. 8:27)

Reading for the Coming Week:
pages 756–840 in the *NIV Bible in 90 Days*
(Dan. 9:1 — Matt. 26:56)

SMALL GROUP DISCUSSION

Today you will spend your entire discussion group time studying one prophet. Depending on (1) the length of your meeting time and (2) the decision of your leader, you will either undertake this study using process A or process B.

Determine from your leader which process you are to use, and then get started. Have fun with this! Some may feel a little intimidated by this process, but our research has shown that, for nearly all participants, it becomes a very enjoyable and educational experience.

Process A

This option assumes that you are one of several small groups that meet at the same location and that you have an extended time (say, 90 minutes) for your meeting. It also assumes that you are willing to forego the video lesson you would normally see at this meeting. If all of these conditions apply, go for it. Many tell us that using process A makes this the most educational session of all.

Group Lesson

Your group's assignment is to develop in 30 minutes a class lesson on the prophet selected by your group facilitator. At the end of 30 minutes, you will gather together as a large group and you will present your lesson to the entire class. Your presentation before the class will be limited to xx minutes.

Your lesson should include the following:

- A visual depiction of at least one incident described in the book (e.g., a drawing on a flip chart)
- Some background on your prophet (see information on the prophets included in Sessions 7, 8 and 9)
- Major incidents in the book
- Major themes or messages of the book

You may use the "hints" on pages 92–94 as a guide when developing your lesson, or you may develop the lesson from scratch. Regardless of your approach:

- Spend 5 minutes reviewing this page and introducing yourselves to each other (if needed).
- Select one person to coordinate development of the lesson.
- Select one or two people to work exclusively on the visual aspect of the lesson.
- Have other individuals spend 10 minutes researching a specific aspect of the lesson (e.g., if using the "hints," assign person A to research hint 1, person B to research hint 2, etc.).
- With the research completed, spend the final 10–15 minutes coordinating the presentation. You can have one person, several people or the entire group involved in making the presentation itself.

If you use the "hints," don't restrict yourself to them, just use them as guidance. Finally, have fun with this. By creating and making this presentation, you are about to learn some things you didn't know before.

Process B

This option assumes that you will be doing this exercise in the normally allotted small group time.

Group Lesson

Choose one of four prophets for your study today: Isaiah, Jeremiah, Ezekiel or Daniel. Look at the "hints" (pages 92–94) for the prophet you have selected. Prepare to develop a "lesson" on the selected prophet that includes the following information:

- A visual depiction of at least one incident described in the book (e.g., a drawing on a flip chart or white board)

- Some background on your prophet
- Major incidents in the book
- Major themes or messages of the book

Then get to work on developing your lesson:

- Spend 5 minutes reviewing this page and introducing yourselves to each other (if needed).
- Select one person to coordinate development of the lesson.
- Select one or two people to work exclusively on the visual.

Have individuals spend 10 minutes researching a specific aspect of the lesson (e.g., if using the "hints," assign person A to research hint 1, person B to research hint 2, etc.).

With the research completed, have each participant or team of participants present their piece of the presentation to your small group. Be prepared to present your material to the larger group if session time permits.

Finally, have fun with this. Just by creating this presentation, you will learn things that you didn't know before.

Isaiah "Hints"

1. What periods are described in Isaiah, and who was the original audience? (See "Putting the Prophets in Their Place," pages 85–87.)
2. Describe God's call of Isaiah (ch. 6). Note that the seraph (singular)/seraphim (plural) are angels. Their name translates roughly as "burning ones." Consider this for your visual.
3. The following passages are often called the Servant Songs:

   - 42:1–4
   - 49:1–6
   - 50:4–9
   - 52:13—53:12
   (Isaiah 53:4–5 is a particularly good summary.)

   What do these passages tell us?

4. Does 55:8–9 describe holiness? What is being communicated by these verses?
5. What is a main theme or message of the book of Isaiah?

Jeremiah "Hints"

1. What period is described in Jeremiah, and who was the original audience? (See "Putting the Prophets in Their Place," pages 85 – 87.)
2. Jeremiah is sometimes called the "weeping prophet." How does 9:1 illustrate this description?
3. See 18:1 – 11 for an important and particularly poignant image. Consider this for your visual presentation.
4. What did the kings think of Jeremiah's warnings (36:20 – 26)?
5. What does 31:33 tell us?
6. Does 29:11 – 14 suggest that there is any hope?
7. What is a major theme of the book of Jeremiah?

Ezekiel "Hints"

1. What period is described in Ezekiel, and who was the original audience? (See "Putting the Prophets in Their Place," pages 85 – 87.)
2. The book of Ezekiel is known for the strange visions described in it. Consider the following for your visual presentation:

   - The glory of God (ch. 1)
   - The watchman (3:16 – 21)
   - The valley of dry bones (37:1 – 14)
   - Cherubim (10:9 – 14)

3. Describe the prophecy of the new heart (36:26). What does it mean?
4. What is a major theme of the book of Ezekiel?

Daniel "Hints"

1. What period is described in Daniel, and who was the original audience? (See "Putting the Prophets in Their Place," pages 85 – 87.)
2. Vegetarians no doubt are excited about Daniel's refusal to eat the Babylonian diet. Do you think there's any chance he was just trying to eat kosher (1:1 – 18)? What else might his refusal to eat from the king's table represent?
3. Many popular sayings have their origin in the Bible. Two originate in Daniel. Describe these scenes and their significance, and consider them for your visual presentation:
   - Feet of clay (ch. 2)
   - The handwriting on the wall (ch. 5)

4. Daniel includes two important instances in which complete faith is demonstrated. Describe them, and consider each for your visual presentation:

- Shadrach, Meshach and Abednego and the fiery furnace (3:8–30)
- Daniel in the den of lions (6:6–28)

5. What does Daniel 2:20–21 tells us about God's presence in the world?
6. What is a major theme of the book of Daniel?

VIDEO NOTES

VIDEO DISCUSSION NOTES

_____

_____

_____

_____

_____

_____

_____

_____

_____

ON YOUR OWN BETWEEN SESSIONS

This Week's Reading Tips

This week we'll finish Daniel, read the 12 books of the minor prophets, finish the Old Testament and begin the New Testament! Needless to say, we'll be covering a lot of ground very quickly.

To help keep all of the different story lines straight, keep this participant's guide nearby, opened to the chart "Putting the Prophets in Their Place" (pages 85–87). The 12 books of the minor prophets were all found on one scroll, so taken together they are about the length of an average book of the Bible.

Finally, as you move into Matthew, see if you notice any significant changes in writing style from the Old Testament to the New Testament.

BOOKS YOU'LL ENCOUNTER THIS WEEK
Hosea Overview

God calls Hosea to marry a woman who is unfaithful to him, and then God tells him to remain true to her, symbolizing God's continued faithfulness in the face of Israel and Judah's repeated lack of faithfulness.

Joel Overview

The Lord gives, and the Lord takes away.

Amos Overview

The Lord sets a plumb line against his derelict people, Israel, sparing them no longer, but promising future restoration.

Obadiah Overview

Obadiah prophesizes God's judgment against Edom.

Jonah Overview

Remembered most for being swallowed by a big fish, Jonah's is the story of what happens when a man's will clashes with God's.

Micah Overview

Micah reveals God's concern for justice in Israel and Judah.

Nahum Overview

Nahum assures the people that God will destroy Nineveh, the capital of the enemy nation of Assyria.

Habakkuk Overview

Habakkuk cries out to the Lord in fear and frustration; God replies that Habakkuk should "watch—and be utterly amazed."

Zephaniah Overview

Dire warnings to Judah, Jerusalem and surrounding nations.

Haggai Overview

God chastises the Jews who had returned to Judah for rebuilding their own homes while his temple remained in ruins.

Zechariah Overview

The Lord says, "Return to me . . . and I will return to you."

Malachi Overview

In the last book in the Old Testament, Israel is admonished for cheating God out of acceptable sacrifices and robbing him of whole tithes and offerings. But, as in Zechariah, God promises, "Return to me, and I will return to you."

Matthew Overview

This first book of the four Gospels (which means "Good News"), Matthew begins with the genealogy of Jesus. He does this to prove the Jesus is the Messiah who was promised.

READ THIS WEEK

Pages 756–840 in the *NIV Bible in 90 Days* (Dan. 9:1—Matt. 26:56)

You are about to read a marathon of prophets. The chart "Putting the Prophets in Their Place" on pages 85–87 will help you recognize key themes in these books.

PERSONAL PROGRESS

If it is helpful to do so, use the following chart to record your reading progress this week. Establish a reading schedule that works well for you—then stick with it.

✓	Day	Pages in the *NIV Bible in 90 Days*	Passage begins:
	1 (Today)	756–768	Daniel 9:1
	2	768–780	Hosea 13:7
	3	781–792	Amos 9:11
	4	792–805	Habakkuk 1:1
	5	805–815	Zechariah 11:1
	6	816–828	Matthew 5:1
	7	828–840	Matthew 16:1

If you are behind in your reading, set aside extra time this week to catch up.

PERSONAL READING NOTES

Take a moment to record the highlights—knowledge gained, puzzling questions, "aha! moments"—you experience during your reading this week.

SESSION 11

READING OUTLINE

Discuss Today:
> pages 756–840 in the *NIV Bible in 90 Days*
> (Dan. 9:1 — Matt. 26:56)

Reading for the Coming Week:
> pages 840–924 in the *NIV Bible in 90 Days*
> (Matt. 26:57 — Acts 6:7)

SMALL GROUP DISCUSSION

 Warm-Up

> *All changes, even the most longed for, have their melancholy,*
> *for what we leave behind is part of ourselves; we must die*
> *to one life before we can enter into another.*
> Anatole France

This week we leave behind the Old Testament and enter into the New. Many of us are thrilled to be at this point—to get past the warnings and failings and harshness and promises—and arrive at the New Testament, where many of the promises and longings of the Old Testament are fulfilled.

If you have read the New Testament in the past without having read much of the Old Testament, you are likely to see the New Testament in a new light during your current reading. You may find, for instance, that *some parts* of the New Testament seem harsher than you recall, perhaps reflecting *less grace* even than some parts of the Old Testament.

But before moving on to our new life in the New Testament, let's spend some time together looking at the minor prophets.

1. "Minor" Prophets: Find the Errors

You may not believe that there are five errors in these five statements. List the five errors and corrections to them below:

- God instructs Obadiah to marry Gomer, a woman God knows will be unfaithful.
- Jonah is upset when he's swallowed by a big fish, but afterward he still doesn't carry out God's directive to prophesy to the Ninevites.
- The book of Habakkuk has nothing in common with the book of Job.
- Haggai 1:5–11 suggests that God does not react to the actions of people.
- Malachi is the last book of the Old Testament.

Please spend seven or eight minutes finding as many of the five errors as you can.

Error and correction #1:

Error and correction #2:

Error and correction #3:

Error and correction #4:

Error and correction #5:

Digging In

2. Starting with Hosea and continuing through Malachi, let each group member provide a synopsis of one book's main message. Allow one or two amplifications from other group members before moving to the next book. Those group members who used the chart "Putting the Prophets in Their Place" (pages 85 – 87) may wish to refer to it. If pressed for time, cover the books that had the greatest impact on your group.

3. After finishing the Old Testament and just getting a taste of the New Testament, what are some of the differences between the two that you've already noticed from your reading?

 **Applying It**

4. Spend a few minutes answering the following questions silently, by yourself: As the Old Testament contained many warnings, is there also something in your life that loved ones or respected people have warned you about, but you've ignored? What is it? Or, is there a warning that came to fruition? Is there any possibility that the warnings were God's way of getting your attention? Any chance you should respond differently than you have in the past? If so, how?

5. In Matthew 6, Jesus teaches about giving in secret. Have you given in secret during the past year? Spend a minute or two silently considering something you might secretly give in the near future. Write this possible secret gift down on your "What Might Be Next for Me" list on page 134 of this participant's guide.

VIDEO NOTES

VIDEO DISCUSSION NOTES

_____

_____

_____

_____

_____

_____

_____

_____

_____

ON YOUR OWN BETWEEN SESSIONS

This Week's Reading Tips

Almost all of what we know about Jesus' life on earth is found in the books you will read this week. One of the benefits of reading the Gospels at this pace is that you will notice areas of consistency and areas of divergence. You may wish to note, for instance, the differences in the four descriptions that Matthew, Mark, Luke and John present in their accounts of the resurrection: who went to the tomb, what did they see there, what were they told to do, whom did they tell? Or, if you prefer, you can use the chart below to help guide you through the four accounts of the resurrection.

Comparing the Resurrection Accounts				
Who went to the tomb?	Matt	Mark	Luke	John
Mary Magdalene	✓	✓	✓	✓
"Other" Mary	✓			
Mary, mother of James		✓	✓	
Salome		✓		
Joanna			✓	
Peter			✓	✓
"The disciple Jesus loved"				✓
What did they see there?				
No body of Jesus	✓	✓	✓	✓
Guards	✓			
Violent earthquake, angel of Lord rolls back stone and sits on it	✓			
Stone already rolled away		✓	✓	✓
Young man in white robe		✓		
Two men in gleaming clothes standing			✓	
Peter and John: Strips of linen and burial cloth				✓
Two angels in white seated where Jesus had been				✓
Jesus	✓			✓
What were they told to do?				
Look at place where Jesus had been	✓	✓		
Tell disciples to meet him in Galilee	✓			
Tell disciples and Peter to meet him in Galilee		✓		
Jesus tells Mary: Don't hold me. Tell my brothers I am returning to our my Father and your Father.				✓

Whom did they tell?	Matt	Mark	Luke	John
No one	✓	✓		
The Eleven and all others			✓	
1st encounter: Simon Peter and the other disciple. 2nd encounter: the disciples.				✓

BOOKS YOU'LL ENCOUNTER THIS WEEK

Mark Overview

The shortest of the four Gospels, Mark focuses on the ministry of Christ, beginning with his baptism by John the Baptist and ending with his resurrection.

Luke Overview

Luke was a Gentile physician who traveled as a missionary with the Apostle Paul. He also wrote the book of Acts. In this Gospel, Luke provides "an orderly account" of the birth, life, death and resurrection of Jesus, highlighting Jesus' relationship with many different kinds of people and emphasizing that Jesus came for all people, not just the Jews.

John Overview

Harkening back to Genesis, the book of John asserts, "In the beginning was the Word, and the Word was with God, and the Word was God." John portrays Jesus as the Son of God.

Acts Overview

Written by Luke, Acts describes the coming of the Holy Spirit, the forming and persecution of the early church, the conversion and ministry of Paul, and the miraculous spread of Christianity.

The chart below gives a timeline of the life of Paul, one of the main characters in Acts.

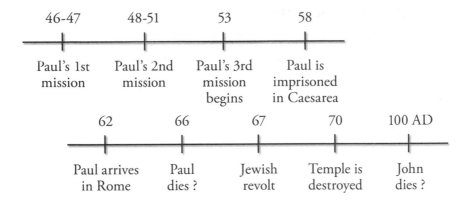

READ THIS WEEK

Pages 840–924 in the *NIV Bible in 90 Days* (Matt. 26:57—Acts 6:7)

PERSONAL PROGRESS

If it is helpful to do so, use the following chart to record your reading progress this week. Establish a reading schedule that works well for you—then stick with it.

✓	Day	Pages in the *NIV Bible in 90 Days*	Passage begins:
	1 (Today)	840–852	Matthew 26:57
	2	852–864	Mark 9:14
	3	864–876	Luke 2:1
	4	876–888	Luke 10:1
	5	888–900	Luke 20:20
	6	900–912	John 6:1
	7	912–924	John 15:18

If you are behind in your reading, set aside extra time this week to catch up.

PERSONAL READING NOTES

Take a moment to record the highlights—knowledge gained, puzzling questions, "aha! moments"—you experience during your reading this week.

SESSION 12

READING OUTLINE

Discuss Today:
> pages 840–924 in the *NIV Bible in 90 Days*
> (Matt. 26:57 — Acts 6:7)

Reading for the Coming Week:
> pages 924–1008 in the *NIV Bible in 90 Days*
> (Acts 6:8 — Philem. 25)

SMALL GROUP DISCUSSION

 **Warm-Up**

> *If you can't believe in God, the chances are your God is too small.*
> J. B. Phillips

Faith is a funny thing. For many of us, it can seem like it changes a lot. One minute our faith seems unshakable, and we feel 100 percent certain about God or Christ or the Holy Spirit. But, if we are completely honest with ourselves, many of us will admit that every once in a while there's this lingering question mark in the back of our minds.

When those doubts arise, we think, "Isn't that too bad? Because if I didn't have that nagging little doubt, what kind of difference would it make in my life? What kind of difference would it make in the lives of those around me? In the lives of those in my community? If only I could be 100 percent certain."

As we read the Gospels, faith is a core issue that gets a lot of attention. In the Gospel accounts we meet various people who could be plotted in a wide range on the Faith-O-Meter. Please review and answer the following questions:

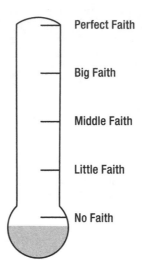

Perfect Faith

Big Faith

Middle Faith

Little Faith

No Faith

1. Based on Matthew 14:25 – 31 and Matthew 26:69 – 75, where do you think Peter should be plotted on the Faith-O-Meter?

2. Can you think of some individuals in the Gospels who demonstrated greater faith than Peter? Who were they? Where should they be plotted on the Faith-O-Meter?

3. Has Peter's faith changed by the time he addresses a crowd of Jews in Acts 2:22 – 24? If so, why? Where would you place Peter on the Faith-O-Meter now?

4. In general, what happens to the faith of the disciples after Jesus' resurrection?

 **Digging In**

Let's study faith in the Gospels.

5. What does Matthew 9:29–30 suggest about the benefits of faith? Does one's *degree* of faith seem to be important?

6. Discuss Matthew 17:19–20. What does it tell you about faith?

7. What does Matthew 13:58 tell us about the consequences of a lack of faith during Jesus' ministry? What does this suggest about the relationship between faith and God's use of his power to, say, move mountains?

 **Applying It**

Returning to faith...

8. (This question is optional. Depending on your group, this question can be answered either during group discussion or privately.) Where would you place yourself on the Faith-O-Meter? Why?

9. How would you apply Jesus' statements in Matthew 21:21–22 to the "mountains" in your life? Based on your reading to date, is there a qualification to the promise in verse 22? If so, what is it? How do you—or could you—apply this in your everyday living?

10. For a moment, try to imagine setting aside all of your doubts and limitations. What would you do if you had perfect faith? If appropriate, write your answer down on your "What Might Be Next for Me" list on page 134 of this participant's guide.

VIDEO NOTES

VIDEO DISCUSSION NOTES

ON YOUR OWN BETWEEN SESSIONS

This Week's Reading Tips

This week you will read all of Paul's letters to various churches and disciples. His letters are among the most personal and distinctive writing in all Scripture.

BOOKS YOU'LL ENCOUNTER THIS WEEK

Romans Overview

The first of Paul's Epistles, this is a letter from the apostle Paul to the early church in Rome. In it, he covers several foundational themes such as faith, life in the Spirit and God's acceptance.

1 Corinthians Overview

Paul appeals to the church in Corinth to avoid division by following Christ rather than competing disciples. He then describes what it means to be followers of Christ and encourages people to give themselves always to the work of the Lord.

2 Corinthians Overview

In a second letter to the church at Corinth, probably written within a year of 1 Corinthians, Paul is replying to an evidently chilly reception by the Corinthians to his previous letter.

Galatians Overview

In this letter to the church in Galatia, Paul establishes his authority before warning the Galatians to accept no other gospel than the gospel of Christ.

Ephesians Overview

Writing to the church in Ephesus, Paul focuses on unity in Christ and living as children of God.

Philippians Overview

Paul's core message to the church in Philippi is to imitate Christ's humility.

Colossians Overview

Paul writes to the church in Colosse regarding rules for holy living.

1 Thessalonians Overview

Following an positive report from Timothy about the church of the Thessalonians, Paul writes to encourage them to continue strong in their faith.

2 Thessalonians Overview

Writing soon after the first letter, Paul reiterates that the Thessalonians should stand firm and not be alarmed by false prophecies.

1 Timothy Overview

Paul writes to his protégé Timothy to instruct him in his leadership while in Ephesus.

2 Timothy Overview

Paul encourages Timothy to preach the Word, since "all Scripture is God-breathed," and prepares Christians to be "thoroughly equipped for every good work."

Titus Overview

Writing to another young disciple, Paul gives him qualifications for ordaining church elders and instructions on what must be taught to a variety of groups.

Philemon Overview

In this brief letter to his friend Philemon, Paul asks him to free his slave Onesimus and charge anything Onesimus owes Philemon to Paul.

READ THIS WEEK

Pages 924–1008 in the *NIV Bible in 90 Days* (Acts 6:8 — Philem. 25)

PERSONAL PROGRESS

If it is helpful to do so, use the following chart to record your reading progress this week. Establish a reading schedule that works well for you — then stick with it.

✓	Day	Pages in the *NIV Bible in 90 Days*	Passage begins:
	1 (Today)	924–936	Acts 6:8
	2	936–948	Acts 16:38
	3	948–960	Acts 28:17
	4	960–972	Romans 15:1
	5	972–984	1 Corinthians 15:1
	6	984–996	Galatians 3:26
	7	997–1008	1 Thessalonians 1:1

If you are behind in your reading, set aside extra time this week to catch up.

PERSONAL READING NOTES

Take a moment to record the highlights — knowledge gained, puzzling questions, "aha! moments" — you experience during your reading this week.

SESSION 13

READING OUTLINE

Discuss Today:
pages 924–1008 in the *NIV Bible in 90 Days*
(Acts 6:8 — Philem. 25)

Reading for the Coming Week:
pages 1009–1048 in the *NIV Bible in 90 Days*
(Heb. 1:1 — Rev. 22:21)

SMALL GROUP DISCUSSION

 **Warm-Up**

From Children's Letters to God:

Dear God,
Who draws the lines around countries?

Nan

Dear God,
I bet it is hard for you to love all the people in the world. There are only four people in my family, and I could never do it.

James

Dear God,
We read that Thomas Edison invented light. But in Sunday school, we learned that you did it. So I guess he stole the idea from you.

Donna

Dear God,
I didn't think that orange went with purple until I saw the sunset on Thursday. That was cool.

Eugene

Dear God,

Thank you for the baby brother, but what I prayed for was a puppy.

Love, Joyce

Think about that last letter as we round the corner to what, for most of us, will be our last week of reading through *The Bible in 90 Days*:

1. Are you getting out of the reading what you expected? If so, what are you getting out of it? If not, what was your puppy (what you had hoped for) and what is your baby brother (what you are getting instead)?

2. If you are current in your reading, how can you support those who may be a bit behind? If you are behind, do you have a plan for catching up? Have you asked for help from others in your group?

 **Digging In**

3. After Stephen is stoned, the church is persecuted "and all except the apostles were scattered throughout Judea and Samaria" (Acts 8:1). Is there any upside to this tragedy? What are other examples from your New Testament reading where adversity leads to comparable consequences?

4. In 2 Timothy 3:16–17 you read the verses that are at the heart of this course:

All Scripture is God-breathed and is useful for teaching, rebuking, correcting and training in righteousness, so that the man of God may be thoroughly equipped for every good work.

a. What does "all Scripture" mean?

b. Do you believe that what you've read so far is "God-breathed"? Why or why not?

c. What is "righteousness"?

d. In what ways would what you've read so far be "useful for teaching, rebuking, correcting and training in righteousness"?

e. Is there an implication that God is interested in our doing good works? What if we didn't do good works?

f. Do you feel that your reading has made you more "thoroughly equipped for every good work"?

g. What about Christians who haven't read the entire Bible — can they be "thoroughly equipped for every good work"?

 **Applying It**

5. Have you learned any lessons while reading *The Bible in 90 Days* that you can apply to your life?

6. Do you see any parallels between how you approached your reading — in both your successes and your failures — and your faith walk?

7. How have you been changed by your *The Bible in 90 Days* experience?

VIDEO NOTES

VIDEO DISCUSSION NOTES

_____

_____

_____

_____

_____

_____

_____

_____

_____

_____

_____

ON YOUR OWN BETWEEN SESSIONS

This Week's Reading Tips

Good news: There are only 39 pages to read this week! So, if you're a few pages behind, you have plenty of time to catch up and finish on time.

Enjoy the reading, and, as you do, reflect further on your journey through all of God's Word. Then, be prepared to come back and celebrate next week at the final class!

BOOKS YOU'LL ENCOUNTER THIS WEEK

Hebrews Overview

In this letter to the Hebrews, Christ is explained against the backdrop of the Old Testament. The author of this letter is unknown.

James Overview

James is a half-brother of Jesus. His message here is to submit to God in humility. This book is a call to action, with James asserting, "a person is justified by what he does and not by faith alone."

1 Peter Overview

The apostle Peter writes on being holy, submitting to others and living for God.

2 Peter Overview

Peter reminds Christians that he writes as a witness of Christ's life, and he encourages all to actively develop a number of Christian qualities as byproducts of our faith.

1 John Overview

Echoing Peter, the apostle John proclaims that he writes as one who witnessed Christ's life. John encourages readers to walk in the light, love one another and fear not, because "perfect love drives out fear."

2 John Overview

The apostle tells readers to love one another, but to be wary of those who do not bring the teaching of Christ.

3 John Overview

John encourages his friend Gaius to walk in truth and protect himself from evil.

Jude Overview

A half-brother of Jesus, Jude calls on believers to build themselves up and persevere in the faith.

Revelation Overview

The Apostle John's apocalyptic vision is a fantastic end to an extraordinary journey through the Bible. Like the rest of the Bible, reading Revelation once is good start, but further reading and study are necessary to begin grasping its complex and layered message.

READ THIS WEEK

Pages 1009–1048 in the *NIV Bible in 90 Days* (Heb. 1:1 — Rev. 22:21)

PERSONAL PROGRESS

If it is helpful to do so, use the following chart to record your reading progress this week.

✓	Day	Pages in the *NIV Bible in 90 Days*	Passage begins:
	1 (Today)	1009–1020	Hebrews 1:1
	2	1020–1032	James 3:13
	3	1032–1044	Jude 1
	4	1044–1048	Revelation 18:1

If you are behind in your reading, set aside extra time this week to catch up.

PERSONAL READING NOTES

Take a moment to record the highlights—knowledge gained, puzzling questions, "aha! moments"—you experience during your reading this week.

SESSION 14

SMALL OR LARGE GROUP DISCUSSION

For this last session, we want to celebrate together! Talk to the group about your experience over the last 13 weeks. Share big things or little things.

How did this impact your life?

Will you recommend that others do this?

If you haven't finished the reading yet, when do you plan to finish?

Should we offer this course again?

If so, should we make changes in how we offer it?

Is there something that you are changing in your life as a result of reading all of God's Word?

VIDEO NOTES

FINAL NOTE

Now that you have read the entire Bible from cover to cover, what's next for you? If you've been using the pages at the back of this participant's guide entitled "What Might Be Next for Me?" or "Questions for Further Study," review those pages now. In addition, your group may be planning future activities or a new Bible study that you may wish to consider. You'll also find some "Next Steps" suggestions at www.biblein90days.org.

Remember, too, that you have developed the spiritual discipline of daily Bible reading. Consider ways to keep this important discipline part of your daily life.

WHAT MIGHT BE NEXT FOR ME?

As you read the Bible from cover to cover and participate in the weekly sessions, use this page to collect your thoughts about what you may do *after* you finish *The Bible in 90 Days*.

WHAT MIGHT BE NEXT FOR ME?

WHAT MIGHT BE NEXT FOR ME?

WHAT MIGHT BE NEXT FOR ME?

QUESTIONS FOR FUTURE STUDY

    As you read the Bible from cover to cover and participate in the weekly sessions, use this page to collect thoughts about what you may study *after* you finish *The Bible in 90 Days*.

QUESTIONS FOR FUTURE STUDY

QUESTIONS FOR FUTURE STUDY

QUESTIONS FOR FUTURE STUDY

THE BIBLE IN 90 DAYS
LISTENING PLAN

If you would rather listen to the Bible than read it, that option is also available using one of two audio products:

Using the *NIV Dramatized Audio Bible on 64 Audio CDs*, listeners will "read" the entire Bible in 88 days with 2 "grace" days allowed during the period.

Day	Start	Audio Start	End	Audio End	Run Time
1	Introduction to the Bible; Introduction to the Old Testament; Introduction to Genesis; Ge 1:1	OT–1, Track 1 0:00	Ge 16:16	OT–1, Track 19 2:09 (end)	58:22
2	Ge 17:1	OT–1, Track 20 0:00	Ge 28:19	OT–2, Track 9 2:49	53:39
3	Ge 28:20	OT–2, Track 9 2:49	Ge 40:11	OT–3, Track 6 1:16	51:02
4	Ge 40:12	OT–3, Track 6 1:16	Ge 50:26	OT–3, Track 16 3:50 (end)	49:08
5	Introduction to Exodus; Ex 1:1	OT–4, Track 1 0:00	Ex 15:18	OT–4, Track 16 3:11	61:27
6	Ex 15:19	OT–4, Track 16 3:11	Ex 28:43	OT–5, Track 12 5:55 (end)	53:52
7	Ex 29:1	OT–5, Track 13 0:00	Ex 40:38	OT–6, Track 7 3:58 (end)	53:10
8	Introduction to Leviticus; Le 1:1	OT–6, Track 8 0:00	Le 14:32	OT–7, Track 5 4:54	61:53
9	Le 14:33	OT–7, Track 5 4:54	Le 26:26	OT–8, Track 3 3:40	57:51

Day	Start	Audio Start	End	Audio End	Run Time
10	Le 26:27	OT–8, Track 3 3:40	Nu 8:14	OT–8, Track 13 1:39	52:59
11	Nu 8:15	OT–8, Track 13 1:39	Nu 21:7	OT–9, Track 13 1:06	54:39
12	Nu 21:8	OT–9, Track 13 1:06	Nu 32:19	OT–10, Track 8 2:33	49:57
13	Nu 32:20	OT–10, Track 8 2:33	Dt 7:26	OT–11, Track 4 4:50 (end)	59:32
14	Dt 8:1	OT–11, Track 5 0:00	Dt 23:11	OT–12, Track 4 1:30	62:38
15	Dt 23:12	OT–12, Track 4 1:30	Dt 34:12	OT–12, Track 15 1:54 (end)	61:28
16	Introduction to Joshua; Jos 1:1	OT–13, Track 1 0:00	Jos 14:15	OT–13, Track 15 2:32 (end)	56:09
17	Jos 15:1	OT–13, Track 16 0:00	Jdg 3:27	OT–14, Track 10 3:38	56:26
18	Jdg 3:28	OT–14, Track 10 3:38	Jdg 15:12	OT–15, Track 6 1:52	51:10
19	Jdg 15:13	OT–15, Track 6 1:52	1Sa 2:29	OT–16, Track 1 4:36	51:49
20	1Sa 2:30	OT–16, Track 1 4:36	1Sa 15:35	OT–16, Track 14 5:14 (end)	51:17
21	1Sa 16:1	OT–16, Track 15 0:00	1Sa 28:19	OT–17, Track 11 2:53	53:42
22	1Sa 28:20	OT–17, Track 11 2:53	2Sa 12:10	OT–18, Track 9 1:43	52:26
23	2Sa 12:11	OT–18, Track 9 1:43	2Sa 22:18	OT–19, Track 3 1:58	53:17
24	2Sa 22:19	OT–19, Track 3 1:58	1Ki 7:37	OT–19, Track 13 5:08	52:04
25	1Ki 7:38	OT–19, Track 13 5:08	1Ki 16:20	OT–20, Track 9 3:07	51:50
26	1Ki 16:21	OT–20, Track 9 3:07	2Ki 4:37	OT–21, Track 7 5:05	53:18
27	2Ki 4:38	OT–21, Track 7 5:05	2Ki 15:26	OT–22, Track 3 4:11	53:49

Day	Start	Audio Start	End	Audio End	Run Time
28	2Ki 15:27	OT–22, Track 3 4:11	2Ki 25:30	OT–22, Track 13 4:50 (end)	51:29
29	Introduction to 1st Chronicles; 1Ch 1:1	OT–23, Track 1 0:00	1Ch 9:44	OT–23, Track 10 6:05 (end)	52:06
30	1Ch 10:1	OT–23, Track 11 0:00	1Ch 23:32	OT–24, Track 9 4:28 (end)	52:21
31	1Ch 24:1	OT–24, Track 10 0:00	2Ch 7:10	OT–25, Track 4 1:47	52:40
32	2Ch 7:11	OT–25, Track 4 1:47	2Ch 23:15	OT–26, Track 1 2:54	53:32
33	2Ch 23:16	OT–26, Track 1 2:54	2Ch 35:15	OT–26, Track 13 2:49	54:27
34	2Ch 35:16	OT–26, Track 13 2:49	Ezr 10:44	OT–27, Track 8 6:18 (end)	48:34
35	Introduction to Nehemiah; Ne 1:1	OT–27, Track 9 0:00	Ne 13:14	OT–28, Track 4 2:27	60:04
36	Ne 13:15	OT–28, Track 4 2:27	Job 7:21	OT–28, Track 23 2:24 (end)	52:32
37	Job 8:1	OT–28, Track 24 0:00	Job 24:25	OT–29, Track 16 3:01 (end)	41:49
38	Job 25:1	OT–29, Track 17 0:00	Job 41:34	OT–30, Track 4 2:57 (end)	42:55
39	Job 42:1	OT–30, Track 5 0:00	Ps 24:10	OT–30, Track 30 1:08 (end)	39:37
40	Ps 25:1	OT–30, Track 31 0:00	Ps 45:14	OT–31, Track 10 2:07	41:20
41	Ps 45:15	OT–31, Track 10 2:07	Ps 69:21	OT–31, Track 34 2:36	42:11
42	Ps 69:22	OT–31, Track 34 2:36	Ps 89:13	OT–32, Track 16 1:35	45:20
43	Ps 89:14	OT–32, Track 16 1:35	Ps 108:13	OT–33, Track 2 1:18 (end)	43:31
44	Ps 109:1	OT–33, Track 3 0:00	Ps 134:3	OT–33, Track 28 0:18 (end)	41:00
45	Ps 135:1	OT–33, Track 29 0:00	Pr 6:35	OT–34, Track 7 3:17 (end)	41:00

Day	Start	Audio Start	End	Audio End	Run Time
46	Pr 7:1	OT−34, Track 8 0:00	Pr 20:21	OT−34, Track 21 2:07	39:00
47	Pr 20:22	OT−34, Track 21 2:07	Ecc 2:26	OT−35, Track 9 3:50 (end)	42:11
48	Ecc 3:1	OT−35, Track 10 0:00	SS 8:14	OT−35, Track 28 2:01 (end)	41:07
49	Introduction to Books of the Prophets; Isa 1:1	OT−35, Track 29 0:00	Isa 13:22	OT−36, Track 12 3:10 (end)	43:59
50	Isa 14:1	OT−36, Track 13 0:00	Isa 28:29	OT−37, Track 3 5:16 (end)	44:40
51	Isa 29:1	OT−37, Track 4 0:00	Isa 41:18	OT−37, Track 16 3:06	45:33
52	Isa 41:19	OT−37, Track 16 3:06	Isa 52:12	OT−38, Track 8 2:17	45:33
53	Isa 52:13	OT−38, Track 8 2:17	Isa 66:18	OT−38, Track 22 3:55	44:07
54	Isa 66:19	OT−38, Track 22 3:55	Jer 10:13	OT−39, Track 11 1:55	46:56
55	Jer 10:14	OT−39, Track 11 1:55	Jer 23:8	OT−40, Track 6 1:30	45:51
56	Jer 23:9	OT−40, Track 6 1:30	Jer 33:22	OT−40, Track 16 3:42	49:48
57	Jer 33:23	OT−40, Track 16 3:42	Jer 47:7	OT−41, Track 14 1:08 (end)	46:32
58	Jer 48:1	OT−41, Track 15 0:00	La 1:22	OT−42, Track 4 4:59 (end)	40:50
59	La 2:1	OT−42, Track 5 0:00	Eze 12:20	OT−43, Track 1 3:23	61:52
60	Eze 12:21	OT−43, Track 1 3:23	Eze 23:39	OT−43, Track 12 6:19	60:28
01	Eze 23:40	OT−43, Track 12 6:19	Eze 35:15	OT−44, Track 11 2:41 (end)	56:08
62	Eze 36:1	OT−44, Track 12 0:00	Eze 47:12	OT−45, Track 8 2:01	59:17

Day	Start	Audio Start	End	Audio End	Run Time
63	Eze 47:13	OT–45, Track 8 2:01	Da 8:27	OT–46, Track 3 4:19 (end)	48:57
64	Da 9:1	OT–46, Track 4 0:00	Hos 13:6	OT–46, Track 21 0:55	45:21
65	Hos 13:7	OT–46, Track 21 0:55	Am 9:10	OT–47, Track 11 2:11	40:20
66	Am 9:11	OT–47, Track 11 2:11	Nah 3:19	OT–47, Track 30 3:10 (end)	44:32
67	Introduction to Habakkuk; Hab 1:1	OT–48, Track 1 0:00	Zec 10:12	OT–48, Track 22 2:08 (end)	51:39
68	Zec 11:1	OT–48, Track 23 0:00	Mt 4:25	NT–1, Track 6 3:33 (end)	38:12
69	Mt 5:1	NT–1, Track 7 0:00	Mt 15:39	NT–2, Track 1 2:26 (end)	59:28
70	Mt 16:1	NT–2, Track 2 0:00	Mt 26:56	NT–2, Track 12 7:42	59:07
71	Mt 26:57	NT–2, Track 12 7:42	Mk 9:13	NT–3, Track 11 1:42	57:19
72	Mk 9:14	NT–3, Track 11 1:42	Lk 1:80	NT–4, Track 5 9:31 (end)	57:10
73	Lk 2:1	NT–4, Track 6 0:00	Lk 9:62	NT–5, Track 2 8:50 (end)	57:12
74	Lk 10:1	NT–5, Track 3 0:00	Lk 20:19	NT–6, Track 2 2:33	59:43
75	Lk 20:20	NT–6, Track 2 2:33	Jn 5:47	NT–6, Track 12 5:49 (end)	57:40
76	Jn 6:1	NT–6, Track 13 0:00	Jn 15:17	NT–7, Track 9 2:27	56:46
77	Jn 15:18	NT–7, Track 9 2:27	Ac 6:7	NT–8, Track 8 1:02	50:54
78	Ac 6:8	NT–8, Track 8 1:02	Ac 16:37	NT–9, Track 1 5:01	50:42
79	Ac 16:38	NT–9, Track 1 5:01	Ac 28:16	NT–9, Track 13 2:07	55:07

Day	Start	Audio Start	End	Audio End	Run Time
80	Ac 28:17	NT–9, Track 13 2:07	Ro 14:23	NT–10, Track 13 3:27 (end)	59:54
81	Ro 15:1	NT–10, Track 14 0:00	1Co 14:40	NT–11, Track 10 5:19 (end)	59:01
82	1Co 15:1	NT–11, Track 11 0:00	Gal 3:25	NT–12, Track 8 3:49	61:13
83	Gal 3:26	NT–12, Track 8 3:49	Col 4:18	NT–13, Track 7 2:25 (end)	61:31
84	Introduction to 1st Thessalonians; 1Th 1:1	NT–13, Track 8 0:00	Phm 25	NT–14, Track 8 3:01 (end)	61:57
85	Introduction to Hebrews; Heb 1:1	NT–14, Track 9 0:00	Jas 3:12	NT–15, Track 2 1:46	56:36
86	Jas 3:13	NT–15, Track 2 1:46	3Jn 14	NT–15, Track 24 2:06 (end)	59:25
87	Introduction to Jude; Jude 1	NT–15, Track 25 0:00	Rev 17:18	NT–16, Track 17 3:35 (end)	62:03
88	Rev 18:1	NT–16, Track 18 0:00	Rev 22:21	NT–16, Track 22 4:02 (end)	20:13

Using the *NIV Dramatized Audio Bible on 6 MP3 CDs*, listeners will "read" through the entire Bible in 88 days with 2 "grace" days allowed during the period.

Day	Start	Audio Start	End	Audio End	Run Time
1	Introduction to the Bible; Introduction to the Old Testament; Introduction to Genesis; Ge 1:1	Disc 1, Track 1 0:00	Ge 16:16	Disc 1, Track 19 2:09 (end)	58:28
2	Ge 17:1	Disc 1, Track 20 0:00	Ge 28:19	Disc 1, Track 31 2:49	53:29
3	Ge 28:20	Disc 1, Track 31 2:49	Ge 40:11	Disc 1, Track 43 1:16	50:57
4	Ge 40:12	Disc 1, Track 43 1:16	Ge 50:26	Disc 1, Track 53 3:47 (end)	49:05
5	Introduction to Exodus; Ex 1:1	Disc 1, Track 54 0:00	Ex 15:18	Disc 1, Track 69 3:11	61:32
6	Ex 15:19	Disc 1, Track 69 3:11	Ex 28:43	Disc 1, Track 82 5:55 (end)	53:51
7	Ex 29:1	Disc 1, Track 83 0:00	Ex 40:38	Disc 1, Track 94 3:57 (end)	53:13
8	Intorduction to Leviticus Le 1:1	Disc 1, Track 95 0:00	Le 14:32	Disc 1, Track 109 4:54	61:39
9	Le 14:33	Disc 1, Track 109 4:54	Le 26:26	Disc 1, Track 121 3:40	57:46
10	Le 26:27	Disc 1, Track 121 3:40	Nu 8:14	Disc 1, Track 131 1:39	52:54
11	Nu 8:15	Disc 1, Track 131 1:39	Nu 21:7	Disc 1, Track 144 1:06	54:34
12	Nu 21:8	Disc 1, Track 144 1:06	Nu 32:19	Disc 1, Track 155 2:33	49:54

Day	Start	Audio Start	End	Audio End	Run Time
13	Nu 32:20	Disc 1, Track 155 2:33	Dt 7:26	Disc 1, Track 167 4:50(end)	59:27
14	Dt 8:1	Disc 1, Track 168 0:00	Dt 23:11	Disc 1, Track 183 1:30	62:28
15	Dt 23:12	Disc 1, Track 183 1:30	Dt 34:12	Disc 1, Track 194 1:52 (end)	61:21
16	Introduciton to Joshua Jos 1:1	Disc 1, Track 145 0:00	Jos 14:15	Disc 1, Track 209 2:32 (end)	56:06
17	Jos 15:1	Disc 1, Track 210 0:00	Jdg 3:27	Disc 1, Track 223 3:38	56:21
18	Jdg 3:28	Disc 1, Track 223 3:38	Jdg 15:12	Disc 2, Track 3 1:52	51:07
19	Jdg 15:13	Disc 2, Track 3 1:52	1Sa 2:29	Disc 2, Track 17 4:36	51:49
20	1Sa 2:30	Disc 2, Track 17 4:36	1Sa 15:35	Disc 2, Track 30 5:14 (end)	51:20
21	1Sa 16:1	Disc 2, Track 31 0:00	1Sa 28:19	Disc 2, Track 43 2:53	53:44
22	1Sa 28:20	Disc 2, Track 43 2:53	2Sa 12:10	Disc 2, Track 59 1:43	52:26
23	2Sa 12:11	Disc 2, Track 59 1:43	2Sa 22:18	Disc 2, Track 69 1:58	53:14
24	2Sa 22:19	Disc 2, Track 69 1:58	1Ki 7:37	Disc 2, Track 79 5:08	52:06
25	1Ki 7:38	Disc 2, Track 79 5:08	1Ki 16:20	Disc 2, Track 88 3:07	51:51
26	1Ki 16:21	Disc 2, Track 88 3:07	2Ki 4:37	Disc 2, Track 99 5:05	53:18
27	2Ki 4:38	Disc 2, Track 99 5:05	2Ki 15:26	Disc 2, Track 110 4:11	53:47
28	2Ki 15:27	Disc 2, Track 110 4:11	2Ki 25:30	Disc 2, Track 120 4:50 (end)	51:27
29	Introduction to 1st Chronicles; 1Ch 1:1	Disc 2, Track 121 0:00	1Ch 9:44	Disc 2, Track 130 6:05 (end)	52:07

Day	Start	Audio Start	End	Audio End	Run Time
30	1Ch 10:1	Disc 2, Track 131 0:00	1Ch 23:32	Disc 2, Track 144 4:28 (end)	52:20
31	1Ch 24:1	Disc 2, Track 145 0:00	2Ch 7:10	Disc 2, Track 158 1:47	52:43
32	2Ch 7:11	Disc 2, Track 158 1:47	2Ch 23:15	Disc 2, Track 174 2:54	53:34
33	2Ch 23:16	Disc 2, Track 174 2:54	2Ch 35:15	Disc 2, Track 186 2:49	54:29
34	2Ch 35:16	Disc 2, Track 186 2:49	Ezr 10:44	Disc 2, Track 198 6:18 (end)	48:32
35	Intorduction to Nehemiah Ne 1:1	Disc 2, Track 199 0:00	Ne 13:14	Disc 2, Track 212 2:27	60:08
36	Ne 13:15	Disc 2, Track 212 2:27	Job 7:21	Disc 2, Track 231 2:24 (end)	52:40
37	Job 8:1	Disc 2, Track 232 0:00	Job 24:25	Disc 2, Track 248 3:01 (end)	41:55
38	Job 25:1	Disc 2, Track 249 0:00	Job 41:34	Disc 3, Track 10 2:57 (end)	43:00
39	Job 42:1	Disc 3, Track 11 0:00	Ps 24:10	Disc 3, Track 36 1:08 (end)	39:47
40	Ps 25:1	Disc 3, Track 37 0:00	Ps 45:14	Disc 3, Track 57 2:07	41:26
41	Ps 45:15	Disc 3, Track 57 2:07	Ps 69:21	Disc 3, Track 81 2:36	42:21
42	Ps 69:22	Disc 3, Track 81 2:36	Ps 89:13	Disc 3, Track 101 1:35	45:23
43	Ps 89:14	Disc 3, Track 101 1:35	Ps 108:13	Disc 3, Track 120 1:18 (end)	43:42
44	Ps 109:1	Disc 3, Track 121 0:00	Ps 134:3	Disc 3, Track 246 0:19 (end)	41:08
45	Ps 135:1	Disc 3, Track 147 0:00	Pr 6:35	Disc 3, Track 169 3:17 (end)	41:05
46	Pr 7:1	Disc 3, Track 170 0:00	Pr 20:21	Disc 3, Track 183 2:12	37:48

Day	Start	Audio Start	End	Audio End	Run Time
47	Pr 20:22	Disc 3, Track 183 2:12	Ecc 2:26	Disc 3, Track 197 3:50 (end)	42:02
48	Ecc 3:1	Disc 3, Track 198 0:00	SS 8:14	Disc 3, Track 216 2:01 (end)	41:14
49	Introduction to Books of the Prophets; Isa 1:1	Disc 3, Track 217 0:00	Isa 13:22	Disc 3, Track 231 3:11 (end)	44:00
50	Isa 14:1	Disc 3, Track 232 0:00	Isa 28:29	Disc 3, Track 246 5:16 (end)	44:37
51	Isa 29:1	Disc 3, Track 247 0:00	Isa 41:18	Disc 4, Track 6 3:06	45:37
52	Isa 41:19	Disc 4, Track 6 3:06	Isa 52:12	Disc 4, Track 17 2:17	45:31
53	Isa 52:13	Disc 4, Track 17 2:17	Isa 66:18	Disc 4, Track 31 3:53	44:10
54	Isa 66:19	Disc 4, Track 31 3:53	Jer 10:13	Disc 4, Track 42 1:55	46:57
55	Jer 10:14	Disc 4, Track 42 1:55	Jer 23:8	Disc 4, Track 55 1:30	45:51
56	Jer 23:9	Disc 4, Track 55 1:30	Jer 33:22	Disc 4, Track 65 3:42	49:48
57	Jer 33:23	Disc 4, Track 65 3:42	Jer 47:7	Disc 4, Track 79 1:08 (end)	46:32
58	Jer 48:1	Disc 4, Track 80 0:00	La 1:22	Disc 4, Track 86 4:59 (end)	40:44
59	La 2:1	Disc 4, Track 87 0:00	Eze 12:20	Disc 4, Track 103 3:23	61:51
60	Eze 12:21	Disc 4, Track 103 3:23	Eze 23:39	Disc 4, Track 114 6:19	60:28
61	Eze 23:40	Disc 4, Track 114 6:19	Eze 35:15	Disc 4, Track 126 2:41 (end)	56:36
62	Eze 36:1	Disc 4, Track 127 0:00	Eze 47:12	Disc 4, Track 138 2:01	59:16

Day	Start	Audio Start	End	Audio End	Run Time
63	Eze 47:13	Disc 4, Track 138 2:01	Da 8:27	Disc 4, Track 148 4:19 (end)	48:56
64	Da 9:1	Disc 4, Track 149 0:00	Hos 13:6	Disc 4, Track 166 0:55	45:25
65	Hos 13:7	Disc 4, Track 166 0:55	Am 9:10	Disc 4, Track 181 2:11	40:21
66	Am 9:11	Disc 4, Track 181 2:11	Nah 3:19	Disc 4, Track 200 3:09 (end)	44:34
67	Introcuction to Habakkuk Hab 1:1	Disc 4, Track 201 0:00	Zec 10:12	Disc 4, Track 222 2:09 (end)	51:30
68	Zec 11:1	Disc 4, Track 223 0:00	Mt 4:25	Disc 5, Track 6 3:33 (end)	38:12
69	Mt 5:1	Disc 5, Track 7 0:00	Mt 15:39	Disc 5, Track 17 4:29 (end)	59:22
70	Mt 16:1	Disc 5, Track 18 0:00	Mt 26:56	Disc 5, Track 28 7:42	59:10
71	Mt 26:57	Disc 5, Track 28 7:42	Mk 9:13	Disc 5, Track 40 1:42	57:22
72	Mk 9:14	Disc 5, Track 40 1:42	Lk 1:80	Disc 5, Track 49 9:30 (end)	57:05
73	Lk 2:1	Disc 5, Track 50 0:00	Lk 9:62	Disc 5, Track 57 8:50 (end)	57:10
74	Lk 10:1	Disc 5, Track 58 0:00	Lk 20:19	Disc 5, Track 68 2:33	59:44
75	Lk 20:20	Disc 5, Track 68 2:33	Jn 5:47	Disc 5, Track 78 5:50 (end)	57:42
76	Jn 6:1	Disc 5, Track 79 0:00	Jn 15:17	Disc 5, Track 88 2:27	56:33
77	Jn 15:18	Disc 5, Track 88 2:27	Ac 6:7	Disc 6, Track 7 1:04	50:48
78	Ac 6:8	Disc 6, Track 7 1:02	Ac 16:37	Disc 6, Track 17 5:13	52:56

Day	Start	Audio Start	End	Audio End	Run Time
79	Ac 16:38	Disc 6, Track 17 5:01	Ac 28:16	Disc 6, Track 29 2:07	57:28
80	Ac 28:17	Disc 6, Track 29 2:07	Ro 14:23	Disc 6, Track 44 3:27 (end)	59:50
81	Ro 15:1	Disc 6, Track 45 0:00	1Co 14:40	Disc 6, Track 61 5:19 (end)	59:02
82	1Co 15:1	Disc 6, Track 62 0:00	Gal 3:25	Disc 6, Track 81 3:49	61:10
83	Gal 3:26	Disc 6, Track 81 3:49	Col 4:18	Disc 6, Track 101 2:24 (end)	61:27
84	Introcution to 1st Thessalonians 1Th 1:1	Disc 6, Track 102 0:00	Phm 25	Disc 6, Track 129 3:01 (end)	61:50
85	Introduction to Hebrews; Heb 1:1	Disc 6, Track 130 0:00	Jas 3:12	Disc 6, Track 147 1:46	56:32
86	Jas 3:13	Disc 6, Track 147 1:46	3Jn 14	Disc 6, Track 169 2:06 (end)	59:22
87	Introduction to Jude; Jude 1	Disc 6, Track 170 0:00	Rev 17:18	Disc 6, Track 189 3:35 (end)	61:59
88	Rev 18:1	Disc 6, Track 190 0:00	Rev 22:21	Disc 6, Track 194 4:02 (end)	20:09

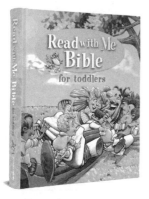
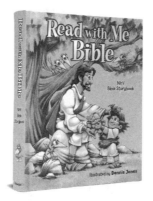

Youth Resources

for the Bible in 90 Days Whole-Church Challenge

Help your preteens and teenagers engage the Bible for 90 days with Bibles designed just for them. Download the youth 90-day reading plan at **www.biblein90days.com**.

ReaLife Devotional Bible
(ages 9–12)
Blue: 978-0-310-71684-6
Pink: 978-0-310-71685-3

Teen Devotional Bible
(ages 13–15)
Hardcover: 978-0-310-91653-6
Softcover: 978-0-310-91654-3

Pick up a copy today at your favorite bookstore
or visit us online at www.biblein90days.com